My Brother's Keeper

My Brother's Keeper

A picture report on the Mission
of the Dutch Reformed Church
in Southern Africa

KARL BREYER

Perskor Publishers

Perskor Publishers, Johannesburg
Copyright © 1977
All rights reserved
First Edition, First Print 1977

ISBN 0 628 01164 4

Set in 9 on 11pt and 8 on 9pt Helvetica Light/VIP
Set, printed and bound by
Perskor Book Printers, Doornfontein, Johannesburg (B315)

man   7

the shepherd   29

the ill and the old   47

technology   61

children   77

the blind and the mute   99

education   109

evangelisation   125

the church is growing   143

prologue to a picture story

With some puzzlement, even a frown, the reader of this book may ask himself why these words of Cain, the fratricide, have been chosen as the title of a picture-story about the mission of the Dutch Reformed Church in Southern Africa. But in Cain's negative reply, 'Am I my brother's keeper?' to God's question lies the explanation. The murderer reacts with irritation, almost with malice, to God's question about his brother, Abel. But at the same time he gives the answer demanded by God: 'I am my brother's keeper'.

And this phrase – expressed involuntarily by Cain – is as old as mankind itself. More than ever, modern man tends to use it often with a shrug and a disdainful smile. Am I my brother's keeper? Today man ignores mankind. This fact is cited as a disturbing characteristic of our time. Tests carried out on the motorways in Germany have proved that a very high percentage of motorists drive past an accident without giving any help. Almost daily one finds people who refuse to take a road accident victim to hospital, simply to avoid getting bloodstains on the seats of their cars.

And how cruel people can be! Like those eyewitnesses in Johannesburg who egged on a suicide by shouting: Jump – you coward!' For the sake of sensation they waited until he finally jumped.

The dead and injured lie by the roadside unnoticed. Man no longer sees his fellow man. Nevertheless, Cain's unheard words – the answer demanded by God – remain: 'I am my brother's keeper!' The New Testament gives a much clearer definition. The Gospel according to St. Matthew says: But I say to you that everyone who is angry with his brother shall be liable to judgment; whoever insults his brother shall be liable to the council, and whoever says, 'You fool' shall be liable to the fire of hell.

Nonetheless, the reader will ask a second question: What has all this to do with a picture-story about the mission? First, this picture-story sets itself the task of inspiring the reader to think – not only about photography but also about the mission.

Photography in our world today – I am not talking about photographs in daily newspapers or about cheap sensationalism in illustrated magazines – reflects a new contact between our mind and reality. In the modern world it seems as if anything defective no longer has the right to exist. Sorrow, disease, misery and death are banished. Man concedes that there are defects in this world, but he does not understand why they have to be seen. In other words, a picture does not represent the truth when it shows an unblemished ideal and beautiful world as factual reality.

Nevertheless, there are many people who demand this misrepresentation from a 'good picture'. However, looking at a picture of today's world is an objective, a dialectical experience. A dialogue with existence is only possible if one accepts what one finds. If it is the mind's purpose to deal with an existing reality, then it may not, for the sake of the dialectics of confrontation, choose only that which is good and beautiful. That would not merely be cheap but also sterile and cowardly. A picture of a leprous and incurable woman might give a person who understands humanity and knows that everybody has only one life, more food for thought than a picture of a beauty queen.

In every modern library, picture-books have taken the place of the novel and of lyrics. Pictures decorate the rooms of the younger generation. To them photography has become a vehement, artistic means of expression, a part of their perception of life – revealing reality with the breath of a new, melancholy poetry whenever words become ambiguous. Language to some people has lost its original power to portray.

It is only a few years ago that the eye of a camera saw the dark side of the moon. Radio photographs – something no man had ever thought possible – traversed the globe to the front pages of the international press. Those who still doubted that photography was an ally of progress, saw their doubts wither away. Ever since we have been able to say that we have seen it all: dolce vita disclosures and mushrooming bombs, coupling manoeuvres in space, the physical hardness of tempered steel, triumphant stars on the stage of the world, and the humiliating agony of a goal in one's own posts – the intermingled anger and shame of existence.

We saw an American pilot trying to land on an aircraft carrier, hurtling overboard and sinking. We saw the Soviet Arctic vehicle disappearing into the ice in a matter of seconds. We saw cameras acting as the harbingers of death. And we knew that those who had died had picturers in their wallets, photographs of their loved ones, conceived in light. Perhaps these arguments are still not sufficient to justify talking about the hour of photography when Christianity and the Christian mission are at issue.

Nonetheless, a scientific phenomenon could be convincing. For the purpose of understanding and making comprehensible events and phenomena of the world around us, the optical representation assumes a meaning which can hardly be evaluated, but which is gaining in importance by the day. Between the retina of the eye and the brain there are about one million optic nerves with a transmission capacity of about 10^7 to 10^8 bits information a second, whereas the ear is linked to the brain by only 50 000 nerves, with a transmission capacity of between 10^6 to 10^7 bits a second.

Our brain receives more than 10 times as much information through the optic medium than through the acoustic medium, and consequently the nature of the distribution of information processed within the brain is weighted unequivocally towards the visual intake of information. In spite of all this there are still only a few people who are aware of these facts and

1

who have recognised the importance of visual communications media. It is shattering to ascertain that we spend years of our lives learning to read and write but not even a second on learning to see . . .

When the Boers set out on their Great Trek in the previous century, they were hardly likely to have been interested in photography which was then just being born in Europe. Before them they saw only the veld, the open African countryside which bewitched them and lured them on. The vast expanse of Southern Africa captivates man and never leaves him even after he had long left the continent.

For those, however, who were born in the veld there is no other home. The veld is synonymous with space and freedom. The sky, the moon and the stars, the wind and the rain speak their own language to those who are at home in this country. In its immense vastness, the veld is like the ocean with which it is often compared. Like ships, the ox-wagons of the Voortrekkers thrusted forward into this ocean. The Voortrekkers did not debate their destination. They wanted to found their own orderly state, independent of British rule – loyal only to Africa. Their goal was before them. Behind them lay the Cape Colony – a mere speck in the ocean – and ahead the unpopulated or sparsely-populated expanses of the continent.

The first forebears of the White settlers at the Cape of Good Hope – 200 men led by Jan van Riebeeck – set foot on the southern tip of Africa to establish a supply station for the Dutch East India Company. Immediately after landing, van Riebeeck prayed to God to support him in bringing the reformed faith to the natives of this unknown Continent.

In those early days the Dutch had no intention of turning the Cape into a colony, but whether for political considerations or from piety, the preaching of the Gospel was part of their programme from the outset. The so-called comforter of the sick (*sieketrooster*), Willem Wylant, who accompanied van Riebeeck, was granted permission to read sermons, hold divine services and to teach the children the Heidelberg Catechism. Imported Malay slaves and Hottentots living nearby soon received their first religious instruction. This "missionary activity" was at first hardly successful. Only after the admonitions of the young missionary enthusiasts, H. Ritzema van Lier and M. C. Vos, that the light of the Gospel should be brought to the heathens, was a greater measure of activity achieved among the White settlers. And while the Dutch built their spotless villages in the fertile western valleys of the Cape Colony, Christianity made headway for the first time in places like Paarl, Stellenbosch, Wagenmakersvallei, Swellendam and Tulbagh. Converts were christened and allowed to take Holy Communion together with the Whites. The religious revival in Europe which, among other things, led to the foundation of the Moravian and Methodist Churches, stimulated the missionary societies. The Moravian missionary, Georg Schmidt, founded the mission station of Genadendal as early as 1737. He was the first Protestant missionary pioneer in South Africa.

At the end of the 18th and beginning of the 19th century the London Missionary Society sent its first missionaries to the Cape of Good Hope. Shortly afterwards Wesleyan and other societies followed suit. The Dutch Reformed Church received these men with joy, and helped them on their way to take the Word of God to the tribes that lived in the interior of the country.

Many of those missionaries were very religious men, who, like Robert Moffat, Barnabas and William Shaw, Johann Leipoldt, Hugo Hahn, Paul Lückhoff and others, had no other desire than to spread Christianity. Others, however, intent upon propagating the policy of the British Government, harassed the White farmers with unproved allegations about ill-treatment of the Hottentots and Blacks. This was possibly one of the reasons for the attempts to hold separate divine services for the different races.

The first settlers brought with them from distant Holland three treasures that were to have tremendous consequences for the future development of the country. The most important was the so-called *Statenbijbel* or official translation of the Bible into Dutch. This translation, comparable with the German translation of Martin Luther and with the authorised English version of King James, permanently influenced the way of life and thinking of the Boers. Wherever the ox-wagons of the Voortrekkers went, the Bible accompanied them. In their isolation the Bible gave them spiritual support and, in practical terms, contributed to the maintenance of their civilisation.

The Dutch language of the Bible was the same which was used for all official occasions. It was the language of prayer, of sermons, of letters and diaries. On their long expeditions through the country, the Voortrekkers were influenced and guided by the Bible to a great extent. In many cases it was the only book which they had to read.

And they read the Bible over and over again. Whenever their eyes wandered over the vastness of the veld and the sky, whenever they were absorbed in thought about life and death, surrounded by loneliness, then the Bible seemed to be talking to those men and women – as though its words had been written specially for them. The Bible brought them comfort and hope and the glory of God was not only a source of inspiration, but also the reason for their existence.

The Boers looked upon the Old Testament as a parallel to their own way of life. In God they found comfort and strength. Without this belief in God there would probably never have been the Great Trek in Southern Africa; nor would there have been any Boer Republics; nor wars against the British and most probably no modern South Africa. The Dutch Bible was used by the Boer families until 1933, after which it was replaced by a translation in Afrikaans – the new language which developed from

Dutch.

The other important religious documents which were brought to Africa by the first settlers were the three confessions of the Dutch Reformed Church which still represent the basis of the Dutch Reformed Church in Southern Africa: i.e. the Confessio Belgica by Guido de Brès, whose 37 articles are comparable with the 39 Articles of the English Churches; the Heidelberg Catechism written by Zacharias Ursinus and Casper Olevianus of Heidelberg, commissioned by the Elector Palatine Frederick III as a guide to preachers and teachers; and finally the tenets of Dordt which were adopted by the Synod of Dordrecht of 1618/19.

Also of decisive importance for the establishment of the Church in Southern Africa was the Presbyterian order of Church government which was based on the Order of Dordt. Jan van Riebeeck and his men regarded the Bible and these documents as the foundation of the Church at the Cape of Good Hope. They became really effective, however, only after the arrival of the first ministers who settled here. The arrival of Johan van Arckel in Table Bay in 1665 not only marked the establishment of the Dutch Reformed Church at the Cape of Good Hope, but also the beginning of the Christian Church as an organised institution in South Africa.

The Great Trek – one of the most fantastic epics of human achievement, sacrifice and sorrow and, at the same time, a triumph of human determination – began in 1836. It is not our purpose to give a detailed account of the causes of this exodus of thousands of men, women and children, of Dutch, German and French origin from the British-ruled Cape Colony. That would merely destroy the context of this prologue. The search of the Boers for a new homeland lasted many years and was accompanied by bloody clashes with the warlike Matabele and Zulus. The *laagers* of the Voortrekkers were attacked and looted, women and children massacred, and

peaceful negotiations with the Zulu king, Dingane, ended in a blood-bath.

In this time of uncertainty, the Boers did not find sufficient time for the spreading of the Gospel of Peace. Only in the evening did they gather for family devotions round the campfires with their Brown and Black domestic servants who had accompanied them voluntarily. Every now and again they encountered missionaries from the various mission societies, such as the American, Daniel Lindley, towards whom they were very sympathetic, and who was to become their spiritual leader for some years. Similarly, the Wesleyan missionary, James Archbell of Thaba 'Nchu, was very well received.

Eventually, the days of the pioneers and the time of the Trek came to an end. The Boers settled down. But, hard as they tried, the young Republicans and new settlers could not find peace. Clashes and compromises with the British Government, which eventually led to the outbreak of South Africa's Second War of Independence (1899 – 1902), brought with them new chaos and misery that left little room or time for organised missionary activity.

Meanwhile the Dutch Reformed Church of the Cape Colony, which up to that time had shown little understanding for the Trek, began to reconsider its responsibilities. But it lacked the men to spread the Word of God. Finally, after a long search, the Cape Church found seven Scotsmen and a Swiss. One of the Scotsmen, Alexander MacKidd, and his South African wife, Hessie Bosman, moved to Soutpansberg, a remote area in the Northern Transvaal, for mission work, while the Swiss, Henri Gonin, founded the first mission station at Pilanesberg near Rustenburg.

MacKidd and his wife died soon afterwards. But his successor, Stephanus Hofmeyr, was a man not only able to convince the wild tribes of the area (through prayer and the example he set of the positive essence and purpose of Christianity) but also to inspire the White farmers and the Church

in the distant Cape Colony to increase their offerings for the mission. As a result of this initiative, the Gospel was also preached to the Mashona tribes of present-day Rhodesia for the first time.

Henri Gonin was not very successful at the beginning and was deeply disappointed to discover that a large part of the tribe in his mission area had left for Mochudi in Bechuanaland (the Botswana of today). He was more successful later and founded the Saulspoort mission station. His associate, Pieter Brink, laid the foundations for the Church which today is among the most flourishing in the independent Republic of Botswana.

In the Cape Colony the first Synod of the Dutch Reformed Church was constituted in 1824. This Synod took positive resolutions on establishing its own mission work. Two years later its first fulltime missionary, Leopold Marquard, was ordained, who was followed by a number of able and devoted missionaries among the Coloured and Black people. A separate Synod for the Coloureds was launched in 1881. In time it grew substantially and produced a large number of ministers and teachers.

Various congregations established by the London Missionary Society, Wesleyan and Independent Societies, as well as by the German mission societies, were absorbed by the Dutch Reformed Mission Church. As a result of this and its own fast growth this Church is among the most vital in South Africa today.

The example set by the Church of the Cape of Good Hope led to a growing interest in mission work in Natal, the Orange Free State and the Transvaal. At first progress hardly seemed sensational, but its activity was methodical and conscientious. The first successful breakthrough came when Paul Mopeli, a brother of the able and cunning Basuto King, Moshesh, asked the Church of the Free State to send teachers to the foothills of the mighty Drakensberg range. It seemed a God-given opportunity to convert the proud Basuto. In this way the

Witsieshoek Mission came into being. It is one of the oldest mission stations of the Dutch Reformed Church in Southern Africa.

In the Cape Colony men like Dr Andrew Murray and his colleagues, J. H. Neethling and N. J. Hofmeyr, were seeking new ways and means of spreading the Word of God, of teaching and building churches. The missionaries took the message from house to house, from village to village, and penetrated deep into the homelands of the Black tribes, until the Second War of Independence (Anglo-Boer War) broke out at the end of the last century and paralysed their endeavours for a while.

The men themselves had to go to war, their farms were burned down, and their wives and children sent to concentration camps. The Boers found their only comfort in prayer and in submitting to God's will. The internment of many men as prisoners of war in camps on Ceylon, Bermuda and St. Helena by the British led to renewed reflection and study of the Bible. Once again the desire was born to spread Christianity and preach the Word of God. Economically, however, the country was in ruins and was slow to recover from the aftermath of the Second War of Independence and the First World War which broke out 12 years later.

By that time the small band of missionaries from the Dutch Reformed Church had done much. In 1891 the Rev. A. A. Louw and seven Black evangelists founded a new mission station which they named *Morgenster* (Morning Star). It is near the famous Zimbabwe Ruins. From here the message of the Gospel was taken all over Rhodesia. Today Morgenster is one of the most important centres of evangelism, education, medicine and literature.

A few years earlier a young minister by the name of A. C. Murray was sent as missionary from South Africa to what was then known as Nyassaland (the present Malawi). Two missionaries of the Church of Scotland were already working in this area on the shores of Lake Nyasa. Murray was given a hearty welcome and much good advice. He and T. C. B. Vlok started mission work there in 1889 at Mvera (Obedience). Within two decades 12 new mission stations had sprung up round a central station at Nkhoma. Today the congregations of the young Church born out of the mission work in the central province of Malawi form the Synod of Nkhoma. Together with the Synods of Blantyre and Livingstonia, they constitute the biggest Protestant Church in that country.

The Church of the Orange Free State was generous in its support of the young missionaries of the Cape Church in Nyassaland (Malawi). Within 10 years of the establishment of the work in Malawi, tribesmen in what is now known as Zambia, were asking for assistance and missionaries for their area. Two months before the outbreak of the Anglo-Boer War, two missionaries from the Orange Free State in South Africa, P. J. Smit and J. M. Hofmeyr, moved to Magwero, where they built a new mission with painstaking labour. It is still active today in rural and urban areas and among the workers on Zambia's famous Copperbelt. At the beginning of this century South African missionaries set out for Nigeria, part of the region known as the Sudan, where they worked under the auspices of the Sudan United Mission. In 1907 two South African missionaries, J. C. Botha and Vincent Hosking, reached Nigeria. In 1911 the South African missionaries were given the sole responsibility for the mission to the Tiv tribe. Over the years 160 missionaries left for Nigeria. A number of them never returned.

With the idea of concentrating its work mainly in the countries of Southern Africa, the Dutch Reformed Church eventually, after 50 years, entrusted the Nigerian mission to the Christian Reformed Church of the US and Canada. Nonetheless, SA missionaries remained active in Nigeria for many years. At the same time the Church activated its work among the different ethnic groups at home. To be further able to meet new and urgent challenges at home, three congregations and 26 mission schools, the fruit of mission work in Kenya were entrusted to the Reformed Mission Society (*Gereformeerde Zendingsbond*) of the Netherlands. In South West Africa a tripartite agreement among the Dutch Reformed Church, the German Lutheran and the Finnish Missions led to joint mission activities.

The mission work of the Dutch Reformed Church within South Africa gave rise to two mission churches for Coloureds (one of them in South West Africa which later united in the Dutch Reformed Mission Church), six regional Synods for Blacks and one Church for Indians. The development of the Black homelands in the Cape, Natal and Transvaal, particularly the now independent Transkei where more than a million people are still ignorant of the Christian faith, the Transvaal Lowveld (about 2-million non-Christians) and in KwaZulu, presented the Dutch Reformed Church with a new challenge. The missionaries of Transkei were faced by vast possibilities and strong resistance. Friendly and hostile reactions ensued.

The saga of the missions continues unchanged in Africa today in spite of the rapid social advancement of the Continent. Missionaries at 17 different stations in Transkei, aided by clinics and hospitals, continue the relentless struggle against witch-doctors and paganism. Today this mission activity, which is partly conducted with the aid of aircraft, costs more than 575,000 dollars a year in this part of the world alone. The grain of mustard seed has grown into a tree. In the Lowveld of the Northern Transvaal the Church has undertaken new projects among the 3,1-million Vendas, Shangaans and Pedis.

Since 1956 six new mission stations have been built in this subtropical region, most of them equipped with schools, hospitals and emergency clinics. In the heart of Zululand near the site where Dingane once ordered the murder of a group of Voortrekkers and their leader, Piet Retief, one of the most beautiful churches in Africa has been built. In the neighbourhood of this Zulu chief's kraal, on the spot where he once drilled his warriors, Black evangelists are being educated today "to fight the good fight" of proclaiming Christ's Gospel of salvation and peace.

In 1947 the Dutch Reformed Church began its mission work among the country's more than 700 000 Indians, most of whom live in the Province of Natal. In 1974 alone the Church spent 402 500 dollars from its own resources on this work.

The full circle is being completed. The first mission stations of the Dutch Reformed Church outside South Africa were founded in Botswana in 1877 and in Malawi in 1889. In 1891 mission work began in Mashonaland in Rhodesia, in Zambia in 1899, in the former Portuguese East Africa (Mozambique) in 1908, in Tivland (Nigeria) in 1911, in Swaziland in 1946, in the Kaokoveld in north-western South West Africa in 1955, in Lesotho in 1957 and among the Kavangos in the north-eastern part of South West Africa in 1961. Since 1967 missionaries have also been active in the Caprivi. From the Cape of Good Hope in the south to Nigeria in the north, the Church has carried out its mission by preaching in 24 different languages to 20 different peoples in Africa.

In South West Africa alone the words of the Holy Bible are heard by the Coloureds, the Rehoboth people, the Wambos, the Hereros, the Ovahimbas and Ovachimbas of Kaokoveld, the Sambios in the Kavango, the Kung-Bushmen, the Mafwe and the Masubia in the eastern Caprivi. From the White Church of Jan van Riebeeck, 10 young Churches have sprung to form a multinational organisation of 23 independent and indigenous Synods.

In the context of the East-West conflict, Africa is increasingly becoming a focal point of world attention. The result is cultural clashes and bloody political conflicts. For its part, the Dutch Reformed Church has done its share towards the realisation of Christianity. It tried to fulfil its mission not for political reasons – although this has been construed to be the case on several occasions – but because it was conscious of the injunction to the Apostles, and therefore to the Church as a whole: 'Go ye therefore and make disciples of all nations, baptising them in the Name of the Father and the Son and the Holy Spirit.'

The crucial step in the life of a Christian is his baptism. Seldom have I been as aware of this as during the weeks and months I spent working on this prologue of this pictorial volume. Although I was raised and brought up in a Catholic household and was, therefore, superficially acquainted with the meaning of mission work, I entered a world to which, until then, I had been a stranger.

Much concerning the mission work of the Dutch Reformed Church was strange to me and still is, but suddenly a single sentence spoke to me as a unifying bond: 'The crucial step in the life of a Christian is his baptism!' From that moment onwards there were no longer any real differences for me, and my work with the camera became more and more fascinating with each passing day.

I travelled from one mission station to the other, discovering more and more signs, signposts on the path of my existence, stories written with a Light of which nobody outside this field of experience can have the faintest notion.

Thousands of kilometres were covered, through the tormenting deserts of South West Africa and the concrete jungles of cities like Johannesburg, Cape Town and Durban. And nowhere was a door closed on the Catholic, the 'Roman', as Protestant Holland mockingly calls him. The doors always stayed open. I shared many a simple meal with Afrikaners who, in areas far from home, preach the Word of God, dress wounds, deliver a Black child by Caesarean section. How different a picture from the one outlined to me about these people. One may question the necessity of the numerous forms of discrimination in this country. Nevertheless, throughout these months, on these endless trips, a picture of a people emerged, piece by piece, like a mosaic, which seeks to change Cain's words, 'Am I my brother's keeper?' into the response: 'I am my brother's keeper!'

The pictures in this book were taken in split seconds. Anyone wanting to add up the total time of the shutter releases will probably tot up a few minutes. Even so it is fascinating that in a matter of minutes, perhaps hours, the whole history of a mission – the devotion of a people – can be recorded. The camera is an unerring witness of our lives and does not need much time.

In contrast with the written or spoken word, photography has a naive simplicity and honesty. The innocence of photography makes it one of the most vulnerable types of communication. It has been accused of being an accessory after the fact of all the things it reproduces so true to nature and with such terrifying accuracy, but this characteristic of photography also forces man to face facts and take sides. Only a photograph has the power of irrefutable proof. War or famine only stir our emotions after we have seen pictures depicting them. Photographs are a 'human document'. They are our life, our joy, our sorrow. The pictures published on the following pages have no other purpose than to represent a 'human documentary' of the mission in Southern Africa.

man

If one looks at a map of Africa, one realises that the Republic of South Africa is only a fairly small part of the continent. Algeria, Angola, Chad, Sudan, Zaire are far larger than South Africa. Even if one includes Botswana, Rhodesia, Malawi, Lesotho and other countries in the south of the Continent, which continue to belong to the missions of Christian Churches operating from the Republic, one arrives at a surface area of 4 754 519 km² with a population of 43 681 739. Brazil, by comparison, is double the size of South Africa and Algeria about half the size.

In Southern Africa – apart from the Whites, Coloureds and Indians – are about 40 tribes of varying sizes, from the Bushmen on the border of Angola across Botswana to the Yao in Mozambique and the Xhosa and Zulu in the Republic itself.

According to 1976 statistics, many people in a number of countries still adhere to primitive religions. Of the 660 000 residents of Botswana, only 70 000 are Christians. There are strong Christian minorities in Zambia. In Mozambique there are now about 300 000 Protestants. In various regions of the Southern Continent there are still people who have not yet made contact with Christianity. This becomes understandable when one realises the distances involved and the routes leading to the people of Southern Africa.

In South Africa which is counted among the world's leading industrial nations, there are, according to the latest estimates, 4,7-m Xhosas, 4,8-m Zulu, 574 000 Swazi, 1,9-m Pedi, 2,04-m Tswana, 1,6-m South Sotho, 791 000 Shangaan/Tsonga, 437 000 Venda and 414 000 Ndebele. Of these, according to official figures, more than 6-million are members of Christian churches. About 2,2-million belong to the so-called African Independent Churches. In South Africa, 73,8 % of the population is Christian, (including the 4-million Whites) and 26,2 % is non-Christian. About 5-million Black Africans form the largest non-Christian group. Of the 2,3-m Coloureds, about 28,35 % (573 400 people) are members of the Dutch Reformed Church.

The statistical picture is overwhelming but only gives a fleeting impression. And the results of Christian missionary work can hardly be calculated in figures and statistics. But a review of the numbers and names of the nations may inspire one to consider the enormous task which has been undertaken in this vast area in almost a century.

If one returns once more to the original starting point – Southern Africa – one can say, in brief, that to date 1 640 367 people from South West Africa, across Botswana to Zambia, Malawi and Mozambique and to the southern tip of Africa, belong to the young churches originating from the mission of the Dutch Reformed Church. The so-called mother church, on the contrary now has only 1 236 867 adherents.

To the young churches also belong the Reformed Church in Africa for Indians with its 1 309 adherents; the Reformed Church in Caprivi with about 1 952 members; and the Igreja Reformada em Mocambique (Reformed Church in Mozambique) with about 8 000 adherents.

To these must, of course, also be added the mission churches in the former German colony of South West Africa which have been active for years and with growing success among the 396 000 Wambos, 75 000 Damaras, 56 000 Hereros, 56 000 Kavangos and various other nations and tribes. So many nations – who can name them all?

Who, outside the mission field, can appreciate the many sacrifices made to get in touch with these people? Only a fraction of this mission work consists of conveying the Word of God to the people in their own language. In 1976 about R2-million (2 300 000 dollars) was spent on translating and distributing the Bible and certain books of the New Testament. In the last few years translations have been prepared or published in Afrikaans, Djimba, Ekoka Kung, Gciriku, Herero, Kwangali, Kwanjama, Nama, Ndebele, Ndonga, North Sotho, Si-Swati, South Sotho, Thimbukushu, Tsonga, Tswana, Tshwam, Venda, Xhosa, a few Bushman languages and Zulu.

Studies are now being done to prepare translations in the languages of the Kgalagadi (30 000 Kgalagadis are living in Botswana), the Kiwe Bushmen, the Naron, the Bakaukau, the Basarwa and the Siyei. The aim and purpose, however, remains man himself.

In 1961 a missionary, Ferdie Weich, arrived in Tsumkwe, the country of the Bushman. With the help of a Bushman boy he began translating the Bible into the Bushman language with its many clicking sounds. It took more than 10 years before the first Bushmen were baptised.

Today the Rev. Weich remembers those times with tears in his eyes. "Yea, the Bushmen, these hunted people, abused and kicked by all, even regarded by many as being not quite human. They are in the process of becoming God's people . . .

"October 7, 1973 was the big day in Tsumkwe," recalls Mr Weich. "Old greyhaired men sat on one side of the hall which was slowly filled. Then the baptism began . An old man, Kaesce, kneeled uncertainly and trembling a little, closed his eyes . . . 'In the Name of the Father, the Son and the Holy Ghost . . . '"

"And, while old Kaesce kneels on the cushion there, a lump rises in my throat. It is a long road the two of us have travelled together, . . ." said Mr Weich.

On that day 200 people were baptised in the land of the Bushmen. Ridiculous, a sceptic might say, after more than 10 years! But can one express missionary success in numbers? Perhaps yes, if one thinks of Malawi which today is the most fruitful mission field of the Dutch Reformed Church. The latest available figures are those of 1974. At that time the young

Church born out of the mission, had 345 000 adherents, including 130 000 communicant members. There were 35 000 Catechists being prepared for full membership. Every year an average of 7 000 adults (converts) are being baptised into the Church of Malawi.

Sources:
South Africa 1975
Official Yearbook of the Republic of South Africa.
Zahlen, Daten, Fakten.
Der Fischer Waltalmanach '76.
Dictionary of Black African Civilization;
DRC Newsletter, no. 160. April, 1974.
Road Atlas and Touring Guide of Southern Africa,
Tribes of South Africa/back cover.

1   The range of nations and tribes, peoples and races in Southern Africa stretches from the Chimbas and Himbas of the Herero-speaking tribes to the Coloureds of the Cape Province

2 The Himbas (the plural is actually ovaHimba) live in the bush- and steppe-region of the Kaokoveld in South West Africa. Their married women are no less vain than modern society ladies

3 The young Himba proudly bears the symbols of his manhood and eligibility for marriage. But he only obtains the right to marry when he is 22 years old. He then wears a plait of flaxen fibre. After I had photographed him, he demanded money. He argued that 'I had taken away his image'

2

→
3

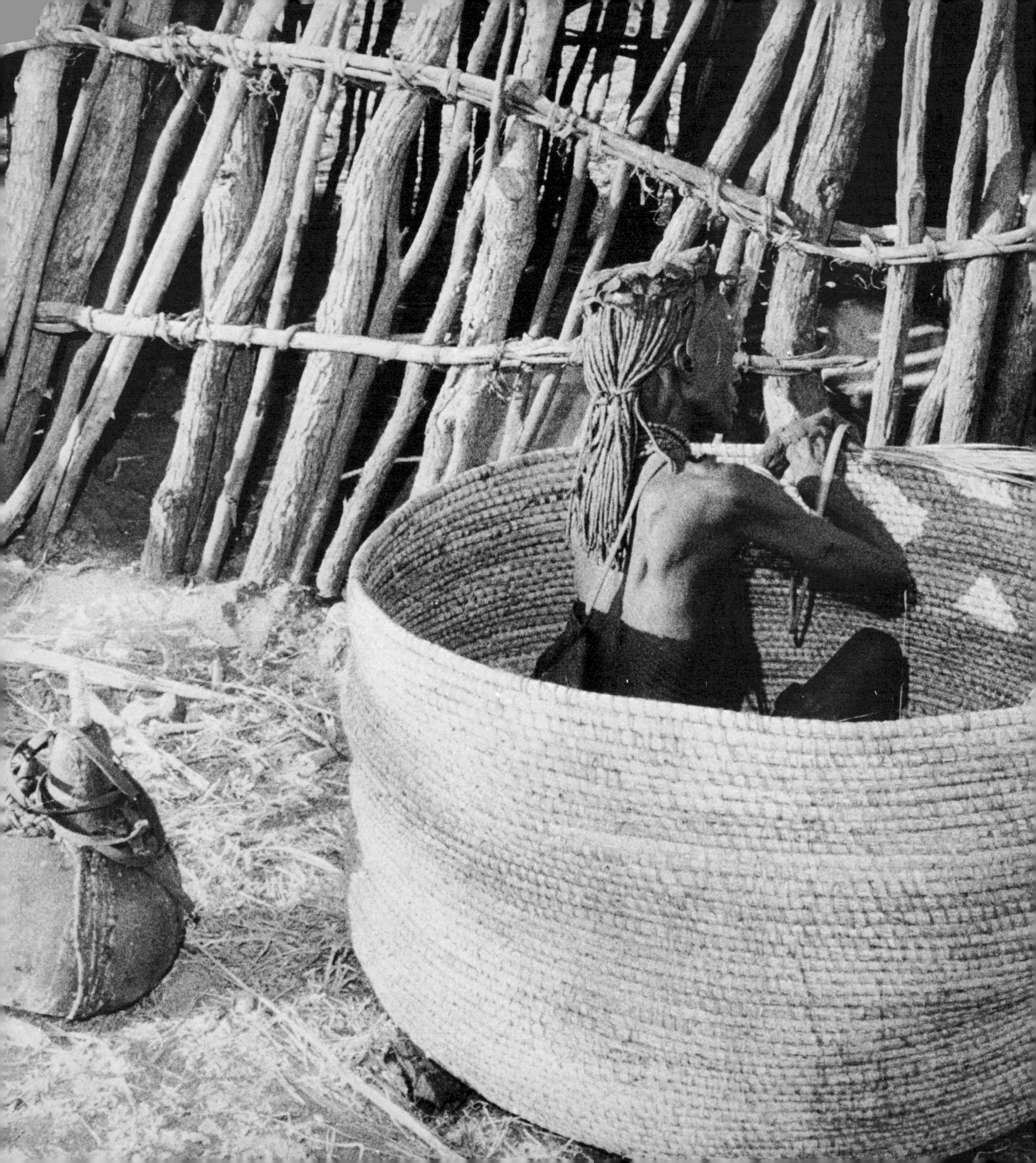

4 The women are born with handicraft skills – especially basket making. On their shoulders rest the care of cattle, simple agriculture, and the repair of baskets and implements

5 Today the Gospel is also preached to the Bushmen. They are a proud, almost sensitive, people, with numerous indigenous laws. They are in a transitional stage between the Stone Age and Western civilisation

←
4

5

7

6 The people of Malawi are at a considerably higher stage of development. The Bible was translated into the Chichewa language as early as 1923. In 1973 the rapidly growing church celebrated its great Bible Year

7 Large regions of Southern Africa are still virtually untouched by civilisation. But even here we already find the kindergarten

8 Water is – as everywhere in Africa – the great giver of life. It is left to the women to satisfy the needs of the family, the kraal or the tribe. And the road to the water source is often long and difficult

9 The Transkeians are among the friendliest and most peaceful tribes in the south of the Continent. Music plays an important part in their lives

8

9

6

10 Girl of the Matheki tribe in Rhodesia which, in turn, belongs to the large family of the Matabele

11 The Sotho of the Kingdom of Lesotho are also happy people with a penchant for motley colours and exciting dances

→
11
10

12 The church at Dingaanstat, KwaZulu

13 Parishioners near Rundu (Kavango)

14 Mother and children in the Republic of Transkei

15 Witchdoctor, master of ceremonies, herbalist – all rolled into one. Superstition and heathen practices still play an important part in the lives of the peoples of Africa

16 Mother and child in Malawi

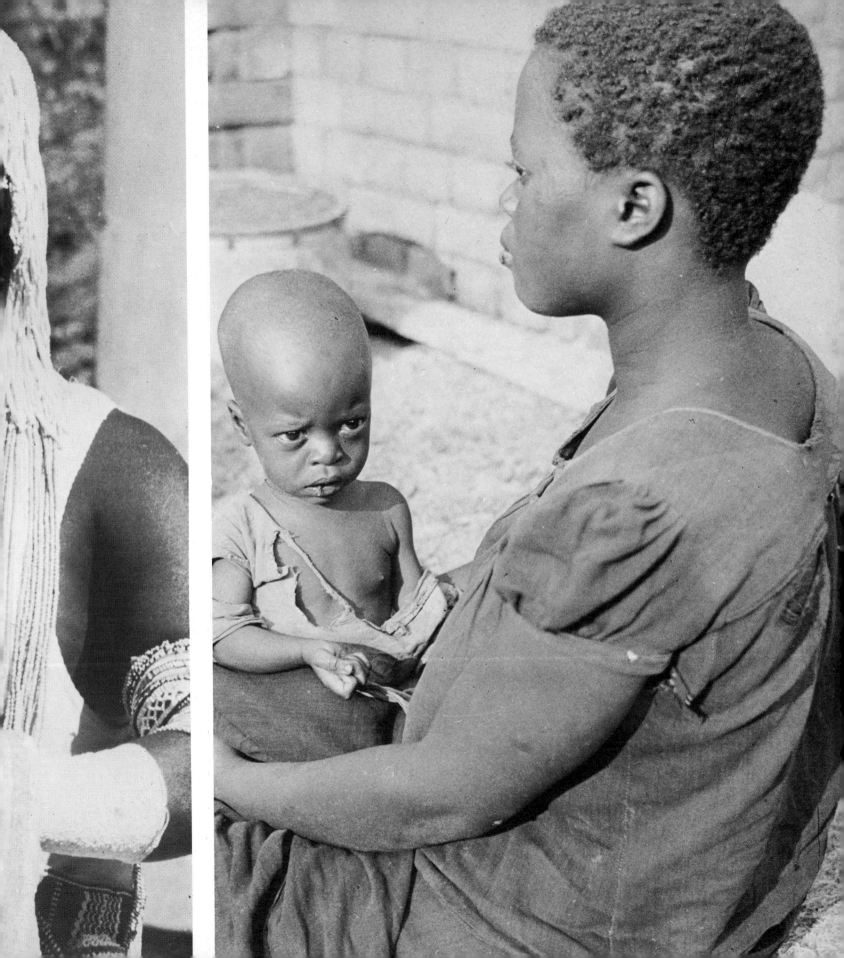

17 Women at a Christian burial in Transkei

17

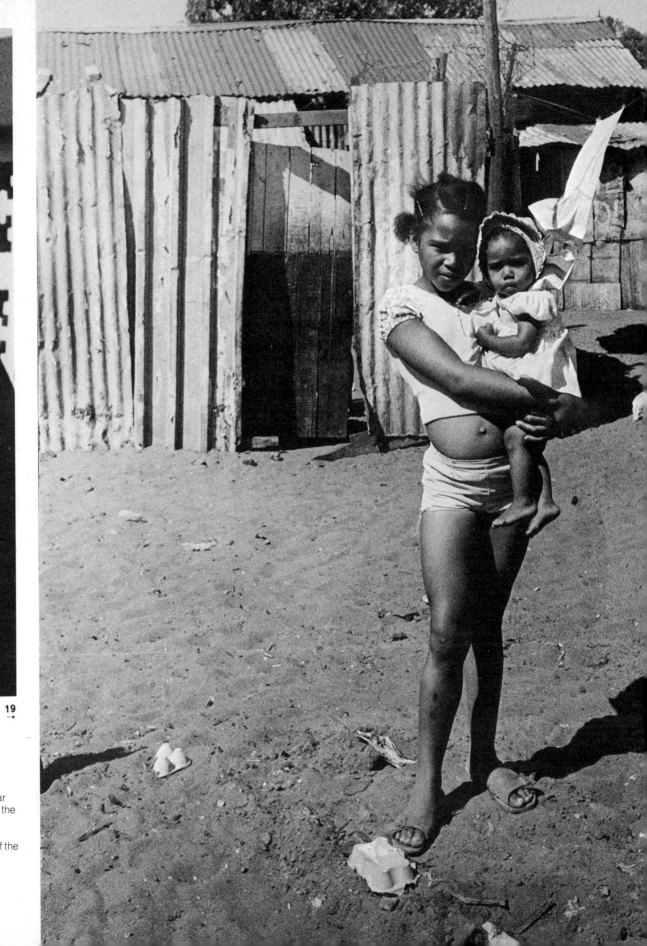

18

19
→

18 Consecration of a new parsonage near
Cape Town, with songs by the male choir of the
Coloured congregation

19 Contrasts in the Cape Province – one of the
four provinces of the Republic of
South Africa: Children in front of the
rapidly disappearing shantytowns

20

↓ 21

20 White and Black ministers at the consecration of a new church in Bulawayo, Rhodesia

21 The Coloureds of the Cape Province belong to the oldest Christian parishes in the country. The first mission church in Cape Town was founded as early as 1799, and the building is preserved today as a historic monument

22 A blind man in an old age home in KwaZulu, one of South Africa's selfgoverning Black homelands

23 Today approximately 87 per cent of the Coloured population group of South Africa (estimated at 2 368 000 in 1975) live in the Cape Province. About 553 000 dollars was spent in the last few years for the erection of church buildings in and around Cape Town alone. In the former slave church *Suid-Afrikaanse Gestig,* in Cape Town's Long Street, a choir of Coloured women and girls sings in praise of God

24 Coloureds in Botswana before going to church

24

the shepherd

They are only splinters, colourful, subjective – KwaZulu, formerly Zululand, Malawi and Botswana. Three mission stations, three reports of events, three times the portrait of a shepherd that characterises many others. But the picture fits together like a kaleidoscope.

There is a celebration at Dingaanstat in KwaZulu. It is now 25 years since the missionary, P. P. Stander, almost exclusively known as "Uncle Flip", was instructed to build a mission station at Hlomo Amabutho. Here also the first evangelists were to be trained for work among the Zulus.

One must know the history of the Boers, the Zulus – and South Africa – to realise the special significance that Hlomo Amabutho has for both nations. Here, near the kraal of the Zulu king Dingaan, Piet Retief and 70 of his Voortrekkers were murdered on February 6, 1838. When, almost 100 years later, a monument was unveiled to commemorate the Boer leader, the idea also took shape for the first time to repay Dingaan's massacre with a good deed.

But Stander and five of his students only began work several years later. Twenty-five years of intensive missionary and development work passed. And now this jubilee is being celebrated and numerous guests are present.

Suddenly a Zulu jumps up and jerks his arms upwards with wild gesticulations. He dances and jumps in front of Stander and screams, bellows and laughs. At first the guests are frightened. But some understand the language of the Zulus and explain. The Zulu is singing a poem of praise, a so-called "Izibongo Zikamfundisi P. P. Stander" (Praises of Rev. P. P. Stander). It is difficult to translate, but in the language of the Zulus it goes thus:

> "Msinaza bethi uyahleka,
> Sigodo senqayi insinansina
> Umambana zimbili zisebhuqwaneni;
> Umkhono ungangowebhubesi;
> Unokhumuzwa bethi uyahlupha,

> Kanti akuhluphi yena kuhlupha umsebenzi.

> Uhlalahlala bemloyisa bethi uyakufa nini.
> Unompunyumpunywana unyamana yenqina
> Ulapha eDingane nje bayakuzonda kwaNongoma.
> Osimelane, noButhelezi, noDlamini, (kodwa hayi mina) Baba!"

It praises a man and his works in the service of Christianity. Among the Zulus it is considered a high honour when a man rises and sings an improvised song of praise.

G. M. van Vollenhoven has been working as a missionary, for many years in Malawi. He is married and has three children – Christelle (7), Gerrie (3), and Riètte (9). Mrs. van Vollenhoven, only recently home on leave in Johannesburg, related her experiences.

"At first," she said, "it required an enormous adjustment, living without electricity and without a fridge, in the bush. Groceries are expensive, and sometimes one has to do with dishes which down here are only mentioned with a certain amount of aversion – the least said, the better.

"My husband works in four congregations. It is richly satisfying work with tremendous spiritual experiences. In any case, I have come to realise that the people in Malawi are very diligent and tireless workers. They are a friendly, calm people and, as individuals and a nation, are worthy of respect. They show a keen interest in the work of the mission, and above all, for the development of the individual. They are very polite and respect others.

"In Malawi," she continued, "one speaks only Chichewa. The Whites are not regarded with enmity and are still accepted. President Banda insists that the Whites in his country set a good example. In this way they can help with the development and education of his people.

President Banda was baptised by missionary T. C. B. Vlok of the Dutch Reformed Church. He, too, puts much value on schooling and the education of his people. Reading and writing have priority on the programme of the Ministry of Education. "President Banda supports the mission work by all possible means. Only recently he handed us a cheque for 48 300 dollars to build a boarding school for girls. I am very happy to work alongside my husband at the mission. Taking over the work in the parish is an enjoyable task – to look after the sisters and to organise the women. I also help with Sunday school and arrange the prayer meetings. Now I want to concentrate on teaching domestic science, needlework and childcare. The classes are intended mainly for adult women . . ."

From Mamono, on the border of South West Africa and Botswana, to Ghanzi and Kuke, live the children of the Veld. They live in poverty, simplicity and ignorance. Here they cower before the assaults of nature and before Tolo, the god of vengeance. Here they search for water, game, a few plants and a message of hope. These are the Basarwa people.

They are Bushmen, but even with their limited knowledge they realise that the name "Bushman" has become a term of derision. They have protested to the Botswana government and insist on being called Basarwa. For the Rev. Lucius Rammala, however, the Bushmen have not changed. He knows them too well. He knows their joy when the rains come, when a child is born or when a piece of venison is frying over the fire. He also knows their fears and sadness. He is their spiritual mentor and he preaches the Gospel to them.

Lucius Rammala was more than 50 years old, in May 1973, when he decided to leave the security of his congregation at Natalspruit in the Transvaal, and minister to the Bushmen. On the advice of the Botswana authorities his work began at Xanagas. Here a tent became his first manse. His five children and wife, Sarah, went with him. Now he has a big house, built by the Mission and Evangelisation Committee.

Today, 42-year-old Verena Venter, who runs the little government school at Xanagas, works with him. She, too, helps to spread the Gospel. But as always, the God of whom she and missionary Rammala speak is too invisible, too transient. And, in any case, there is still Tolo, the god of vengeance, who works at night.

Nevertheless, the Bushmen are interested. If one asks them whether they have understood the meaning of God's word, they nod their heads. To the Black farmers in Botswana, however, the Bushmen are of little account. Now and then they are given the opportunity to earn something: 5 dollars a month and seven cups of maize flour. Also a cup of sugar and a little tobacco. But they are not allowed to sit next to a Black cattle farmer at the same fire.

But the Rev. Rammala is tireless. He built a small, primitive boarding school. In 1973 he had 40 pupils and now there are 73. He obtained money to buy 10 milking cows and build a little farmstead. Here he labours, preaches, and lives with the children of the Kalahari Desert. He reads to them from the Heidelberg Catechism, known here as *Buka ya Dipotso Ya Baipodi*. He quotes from the *Lefoko La Gago Ke Lebone* (Thy Word is a Light for me).

On Sundays he also holds church services and prayer meetings for the older people. Sometimes he reaches more than 3 000 souls and he is convinced that Christianity has a future among the Bushmen.

The Black congregations of the Dutch Reformed Church in Southern Transvaal also recognise the magnificent work being done by their Black missionary, Lucius Rammala. At his induction, representatives of 75 congregations and 75 ministers prayed for his blessing. Many more attended the funeral of his wife, who died in March 1976. When he recently needed financial aid, the ministers in the Transvaal started a new collection. Some could only give dollars. But the Basarwa in Western Botswana know that at Xanagas lives a man who proclaims the message of faith, hope and love. But the foremost of these is love.

P.S.
The most recent figures show that there are 1 078 Whites serving the Dutch Reformed Church Mission. There are also 308 White ordained missionaries, 88 Coloured clergymen, 315 Black clergymen, 702 Black evangelists, 5 Indian clergymen and three Indian evangelists. Nearly all the missionaries and clergymen in the mission are married. The number of unmarried preachers is small.

1, 2 + 3 Nothing is easier than to imagine a missionary in the pulpit. Nonetheless, the spreading of the Word requires constant sacrifice and denial, hardships and labour. Missionary Buys can tell many stories about this. During a trip to the outposts in the Kaokoveld in South West Africa, the truck got stuck in the sand

2

3 →

4,5 — 7 But there are also more pleasant sides to the missionary work. Today it is not only the tribal heads who have their praise-singer. The students at the Dingaanstat Theological College in KwaZulu call him "Oom Flip". Missionary P. P. Stander is greeted with a song of praise about his person and his deeds. The joy among the Zulu students is great. Oom Flip belongs to them, even when he is saying farewell

8. Tree-church in Kavango

9. Consecration of a church in Bulawayo

10 A missionary does not always have a church at his disposal. It often happens – before the tribal chief allocates him a piece of ground – that he has to hold his first services under a tree. Still, the times of the "tree church", as here in the Caprivi, (South West Africa), which belong to the pioneer years, count among his fondest memories

11 The Rev. Barry welcomes members of his congregation in Mochudi (Botswana)

12 Reverend O. A. Cloete reads from the Bible to the women of Dimbaza, in the Ciskei, one of the Black homelands in South Africa, where the church built a modern factory with aid by Zipha

13 A factory can álso become a church

11

12

13
→

14 The Rev. Magwegwe Mandebvu addresses his congregation during the consecration of a new church in Bulawayo

15 The Rev. E. N. Casaleggio at Saulspoort (Transvaal) is an experienced worker in the mission field. For years he worked in the Dutch Reformed Mission in Nigeria. Today he is in charge of one of the oldest missions in the Transvaal

16 Meeting of the church elders in a congregation in Malawi. The discussions are extremely lively, a sign of the congregation's keen participation in the life of the church. Malawi rightfully belongs to the most fruitful missions in Southern Africa

17

18

19 →

20

21

22

17, 18, 19, 20, 21 + 22 A happy family man and one of the most active ministers of the Indian Mission, the Rev. S. Govender of Durban. Today there are two congregations of the (Indian) Reformed Church in Africa in this harbour city. He, three mission ministers and two Indian evangelists see to it that the Word of God is spread

23

24 ↓

23, 24 + 25 Missionary F. H. Weich has been working among the Bushmen since 1961. 'I arrived here (Tsumkwe, South West Africa) on a Friday afternoon', he recalls. 'It was very hot in the tent. I began building a hut of grass.' And four years later 'I met some Bushmen at a place called !Xog!u (Elephantwater) I wanted to tell them the Glad Tiding, but I had no translator. Forced by circumstances and reborn by mercy I preached and prayed in the Bushman language for the first time in my life . . .' (July 26, 1965)

26 + 27 At Takuasa, near Rundu, in South West Africa, a missionary has assembled his helpers and evangelists for prayer and discussions. Only a humble classroom is available

28 'Go therefore and make disciples of all nations, baptising them in the Name of the Father and of the Son and of the Holy Spirit.' A baptism in Malawi

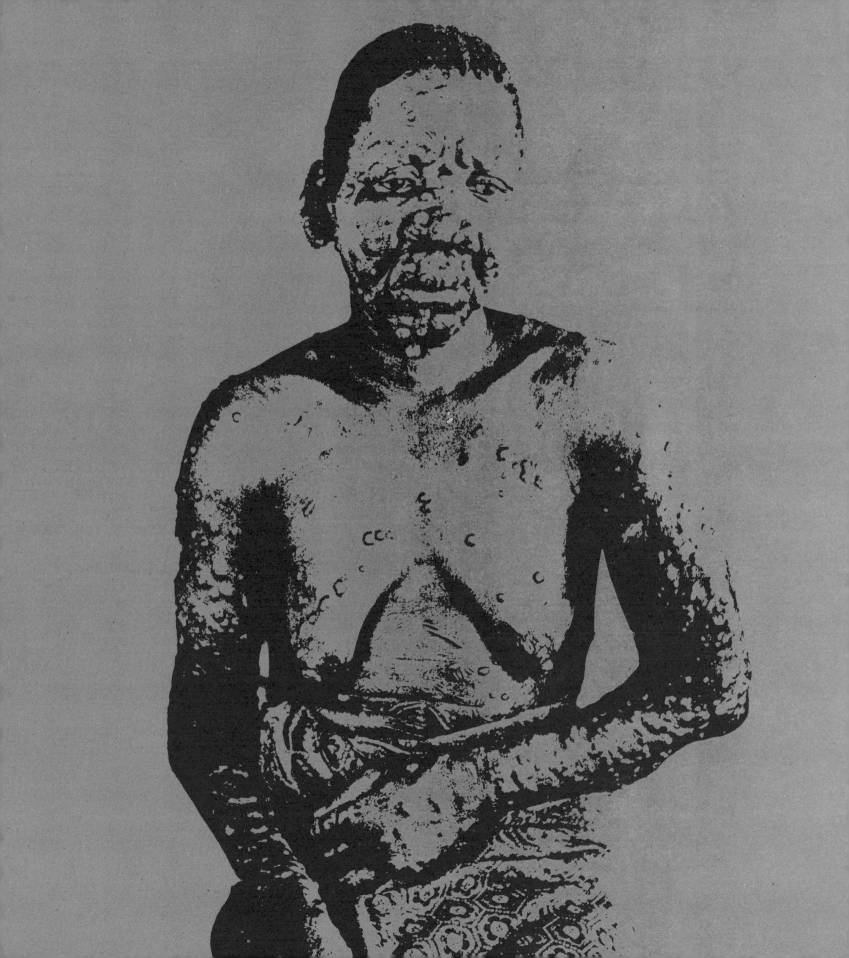

the ill and the old

The first missionaries knew that helping the aged and ill was one way to proclaim the Gospel. The mission hospital or the primitive hut rebuilt into a clinic in the bush was often the first meeting place of Christianity and paganism – the first opportunity to proclaim the Word of God. But even at this meeting a series of tremendous obstacles, especially from the witchdoctor's side, had to be overcome. Today the witchdoctor, whose influence is even growing in the modern societies of the Black people in Southern Africa, is still the biggest obstacle in the work of the mission.

In addition, the Black African's concept of illness and physical suffering is closely related to his beliefs about religion, gods and ancestor cults. Pain, sickness and suffering are, in short, the negative result of the connections between the dead and their descendants or caused by living malefactors. It would be beyond the scope of this report to explain the backgrounds, thought processes and deep meanings of the ancestor cult and religious beliefs which would actually be necessary to understand the attitude of the Black African to suffering, illness and death.

If someone dies, the Zulu resignedly declares: "Ubiziwe abaphansi" (the ancestors have called him.) When the people are beset by sickness, "abaphansi basifulethele!" – the ancestors have turned their backs on us.) The diviner, *isangoma*, must establish the causes and prescribe what sacrifices must be made to purge the community again. The fight against this superstition has lasted for years and will yet last for a great number of years.

But one must not forget that other nations also took their time to overcome their pagan, magical beliefs. In the years to come the Black African in Southern Africa will surely spend enormous sums of money to pay the witchdoctor – the *intelezi*, who protects his home against magicians and witches. He will buy bracelets to keep away sickness and pain and charms to protect him against lightning and disasters. But eventually the Black people of this continent will realise that one can combat illness and suffering when one knows their causes and when one has substituted scientific arguments for the theories about spirits and ancestors.

The missionaries of the Dutch Reformed Church have, over the years, established a closely knit net of hospitals and clinics over this part of the Continent. From Letaba, on the banks of the Letaba river, from Tzaneen, via Tshilidzini to the most modern clinics and hospitals in Transkei, there is today a row of establishments that would be the envy of European doctors and patients. Over the years doctors and nursing aides, sisters and officials have sacrificed themselves for the Black sick and old.

In the meantime the South African Government has recognised that the healing of the sick is one of the modern state's greatest tasks. It has also realised that the Church is asked to heal one's fellow man. That is why today the mission receives increasing aid in medicine. In many parts of South Africa hospitals are being built by the Church, but are financed wholly or partly by die State. Lately they have been transferred to the civil authorities of the Black homelands.

In this way the Church is able to carry out Christ's command effectively and speedily. There is the danger however, that many modern and well equipped hospitals have not enough staff. There are not sufficient numbers of people interested in this type of calling.

Since 1974 plans have been made to hand over 30 newly built mission hospitals to the state. These hospitals have a total of 8 991 beds. Up to the time of writing, 123 362 patients a year had been treated in these 30 hospitals. In addition 950 634 ambulant treatments have been carried out.

Outside South Africa, a total of 10 hospitals with 791 beds have been handed to the young Churches of the Dutch Reformed Church Mission in various countries. Previously they were organised and administered by the Dutch Reformed Church. The hospitals are in Rhodesia (2), Malawi (5), Zambia (2) and Botswana (1).

These hospitals have so far treated 22 766 internal patients and 134 994 outpatients a year. In Southern Africa the missions of the Dutch Reformed Church also have 11 establishments for old people and chronically ill patients, five homes for cerebral palsied patients, two establishments for epileptics, a home for unmarried mothers, and an establishment for people who have been treated for leprosy and were discharged. There are special departments for mentally ill people at several of these hospitals.

The costs of the hospitals in South Africa are being met by the Government. At mission hospitals outside South Africa the Government concerned pays 50 % to 80 % of the running costs and only in some cases the total costs for the erection of new buildings and medical institutions. The entire mission work is being financed by the regional synods of the Dutch Reformed Church in South Africa. The different Synods spend a specified sum, according to the extent of the mission work done by the Synod concerned. The three Synods of the Transvaal alone spend about 3 900 000 dollars a year on mission work. Natal spent 355 500 dollars, the two Synods of the Cape 2 990 000 dollars, and the Orange Free State spent 2 300 000 dollars. That means that the Synods of the Dutch Reformed Church have spent a total of more than R8 million (0.5 million dollar) i.e. R10 a member.

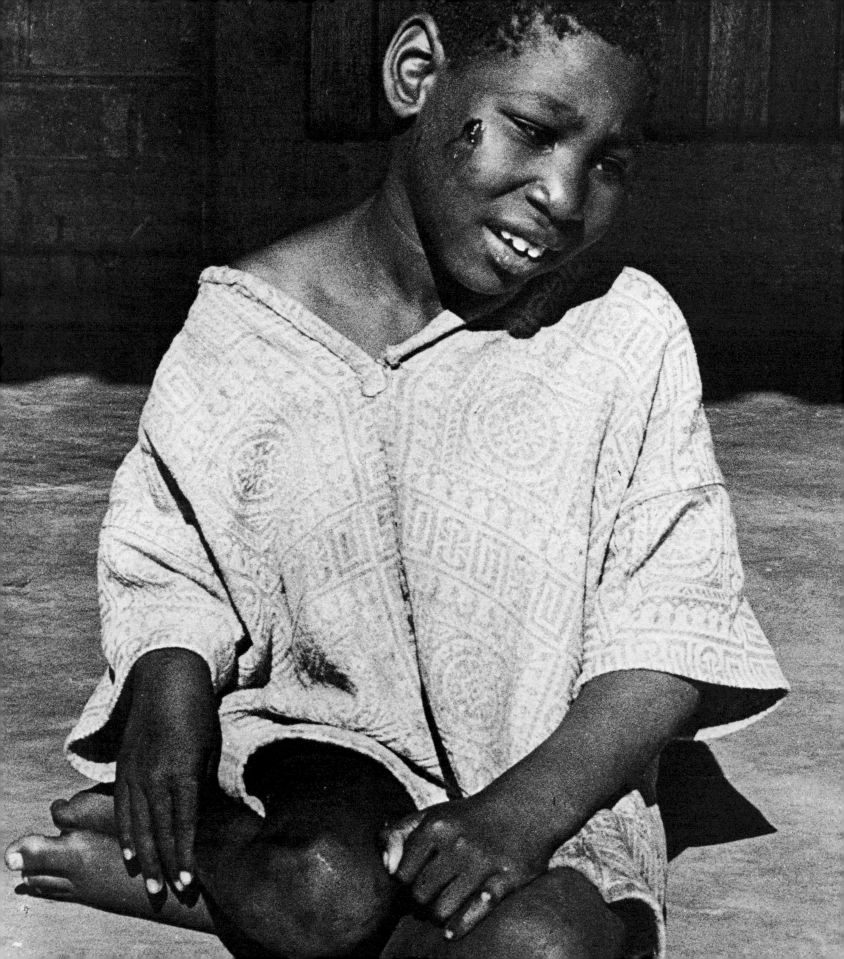

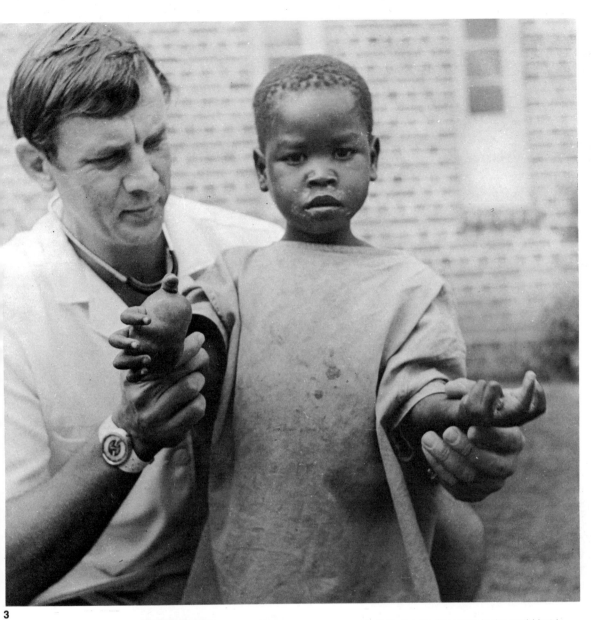

3

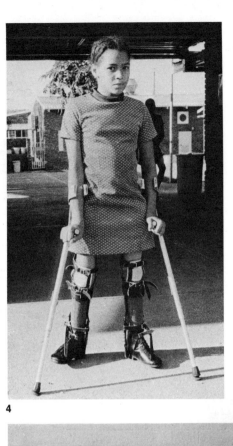

4

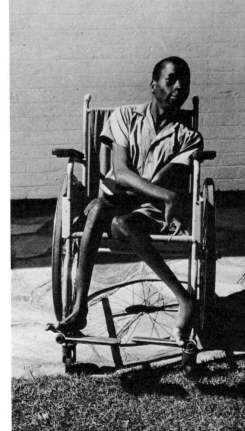

2

1, 2, 3, 4 + 5 Nowhere in the world but in Africa are ailing and old people so alone. The tribes on the Continent know little about caring for suffering humanity who have to rely on themselves. One of the most important tasks of the mission is to alleviate hardship and to help people who are old, ill and crippled. From Letaba in the Transvaal down to Kwabadala in KwaZulu (Zululand) the D. R. Church has built a number of homes in which the ailing, crippled and old are being cared for, and for whom "life is again worth living"

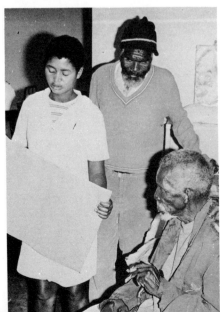

←
1

5

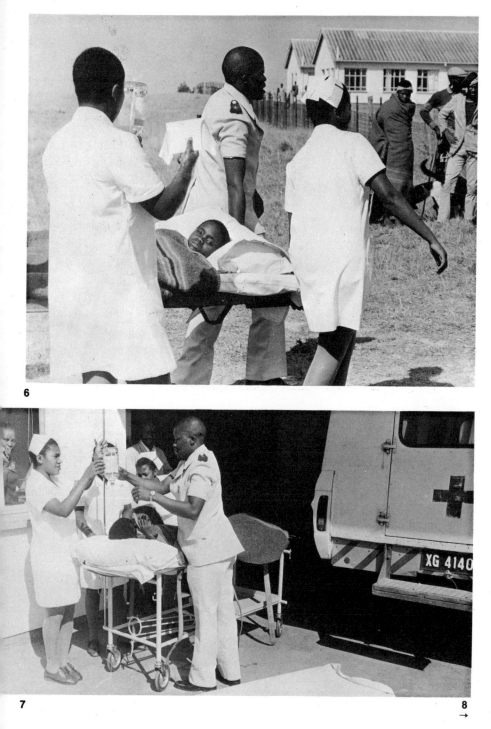

6

7

8
→

10

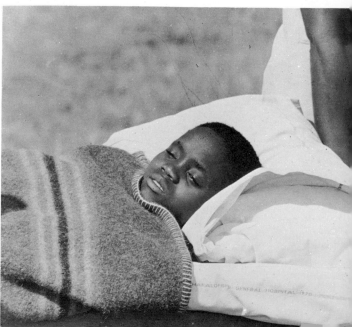

6, 7 + 8 An aircraft of the Missionary Aviation Fellowship, bringing an ailing boy, lands at Thafalofefe in Transkei. Nurses carry him into one of the most modern hospitals in Southern Africa

9 + 10 At Kwabadala in KwaZulu an old man, who does not know where he comes from or to whom he belongs, is being cared for by a doctor and nurses

9
→

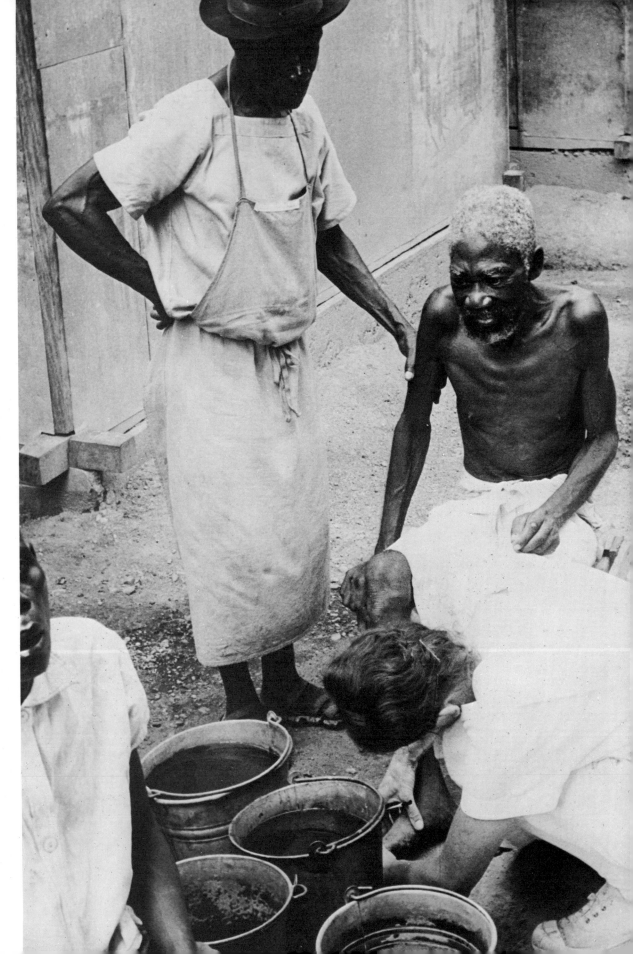

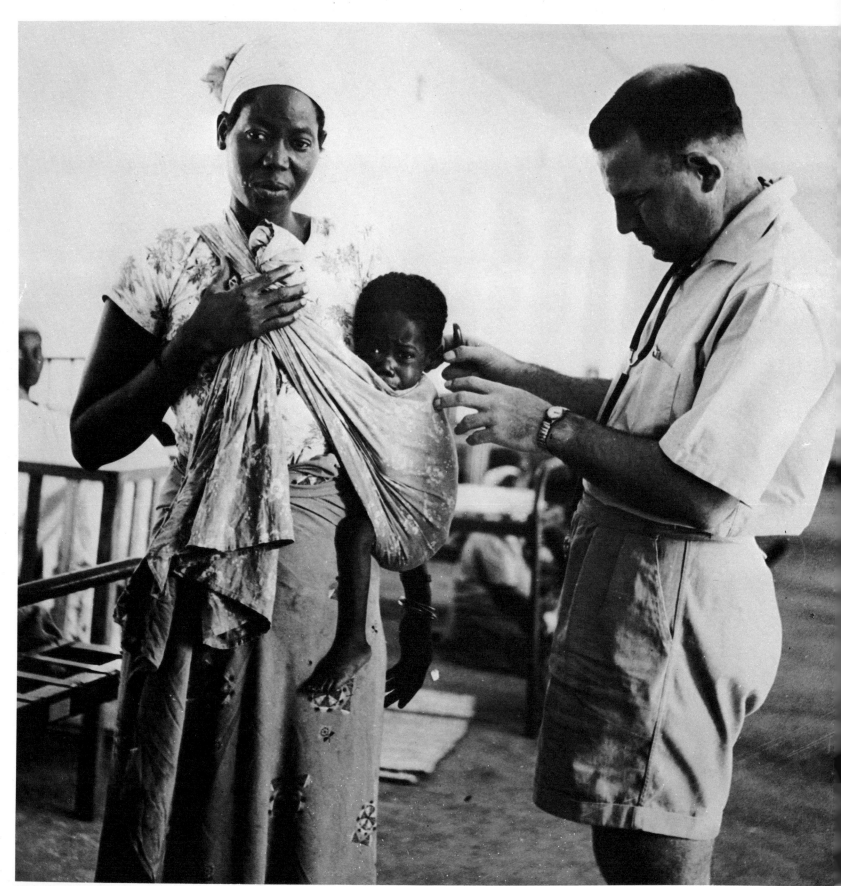

13

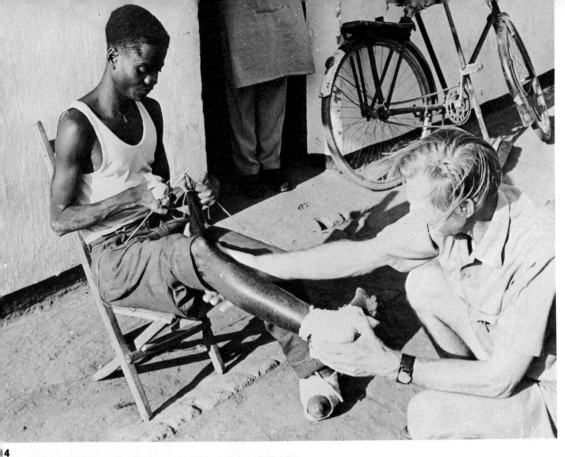

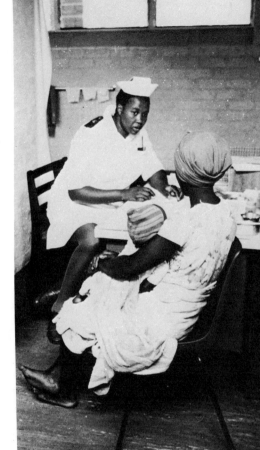

11 Black and White nurses treat a patient

12 In numerous mission regions the hospitals also have outstations where experienced nurses treat the sick walking from the bush

13, 14 + 15 Dedicated White doctors - men and women - look after Black patients, as here in Malawi . . . and in Mochudi (Botswana)

12

15

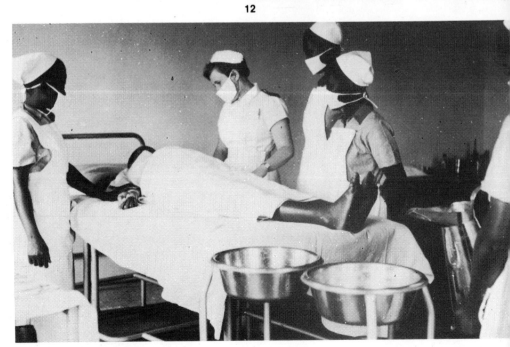

11

53

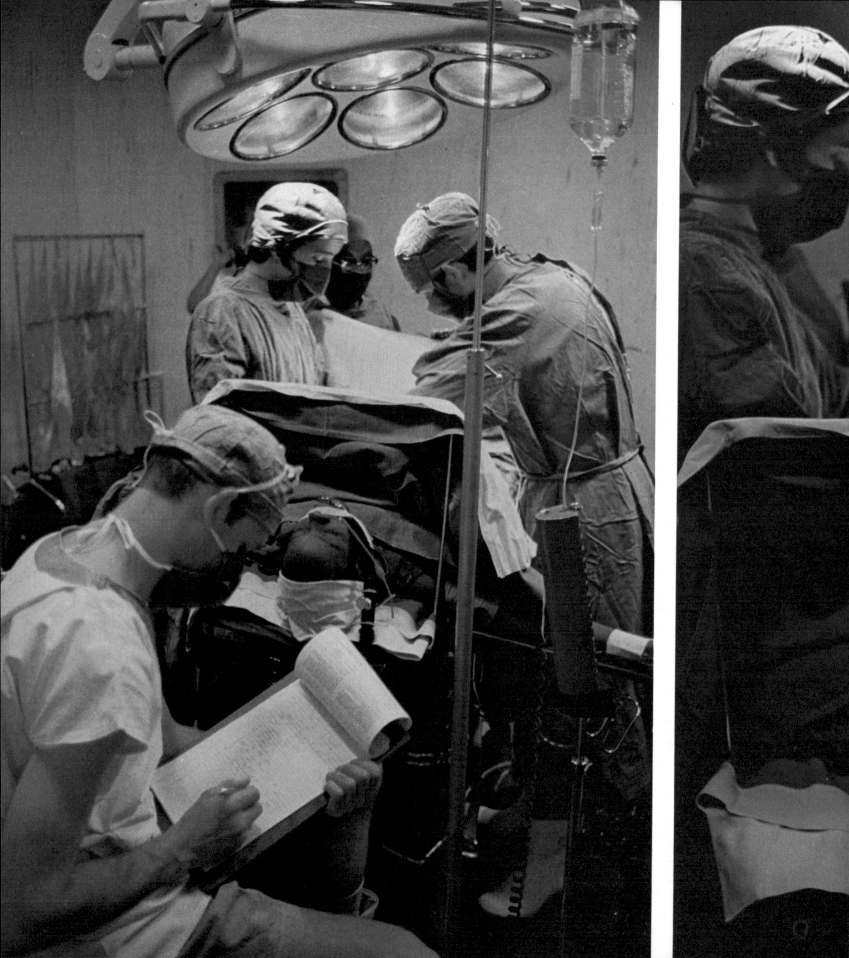

16 ← ←

← 17

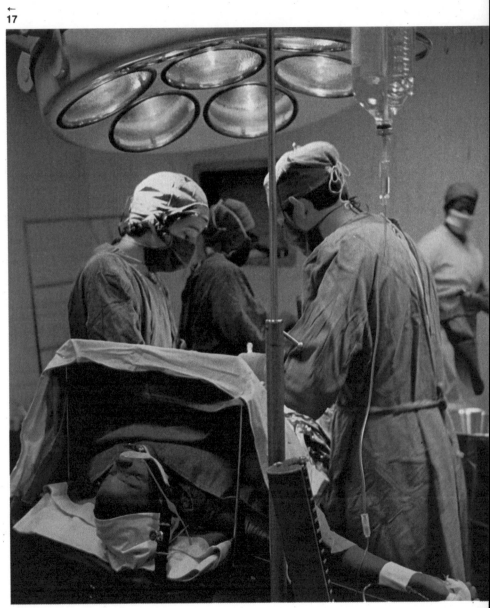

18

16, 17 + 18 A Caesarian operation in the hospital at Tshilidzini

55

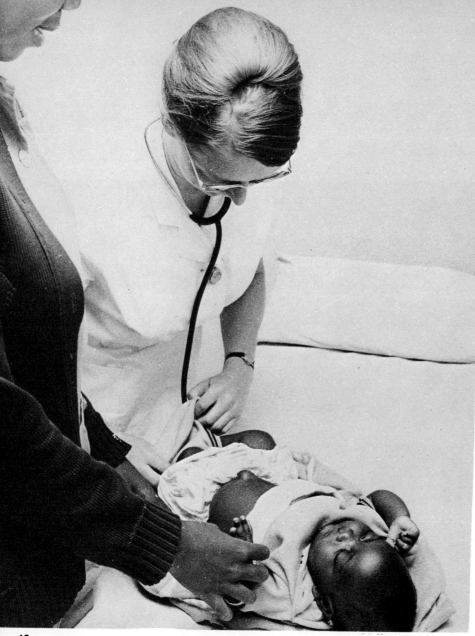

19

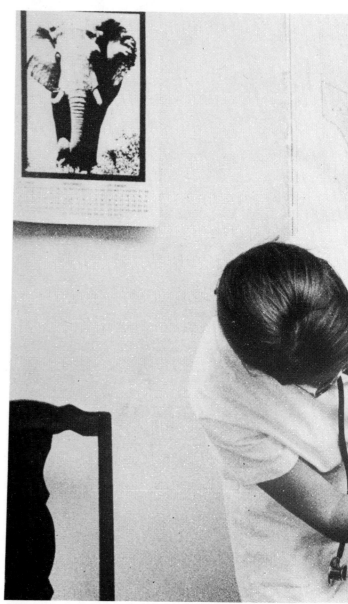

20

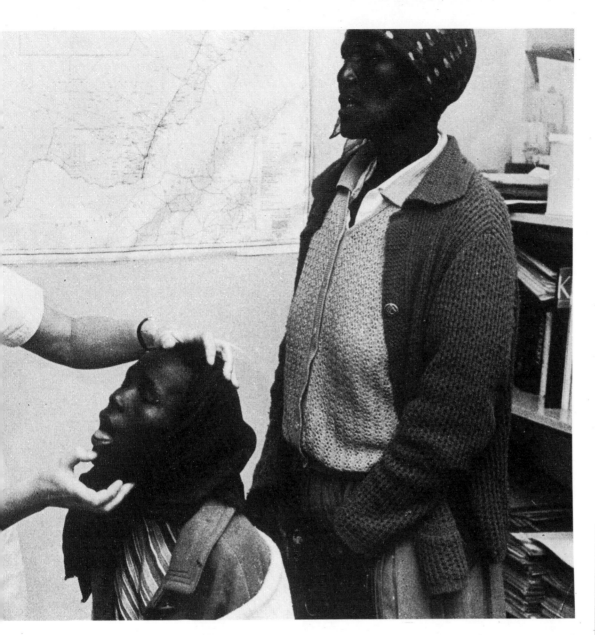

19 + 20 Well-trained nurses are at hand.
The Black doctors, however, are rarely
interested in medical mission work

21 + 22 At Opuwo in the Kaokoveld of South
West Africa and at Kwabadala in KwaZulu the
elderly enjoy the day in their own fashion. The
mission station of the D. R. Church has become
their home

21

22
←

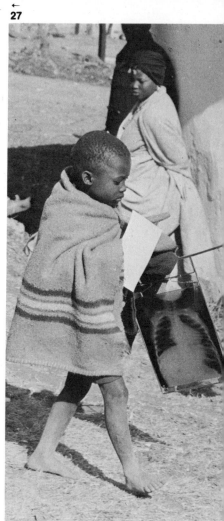

24

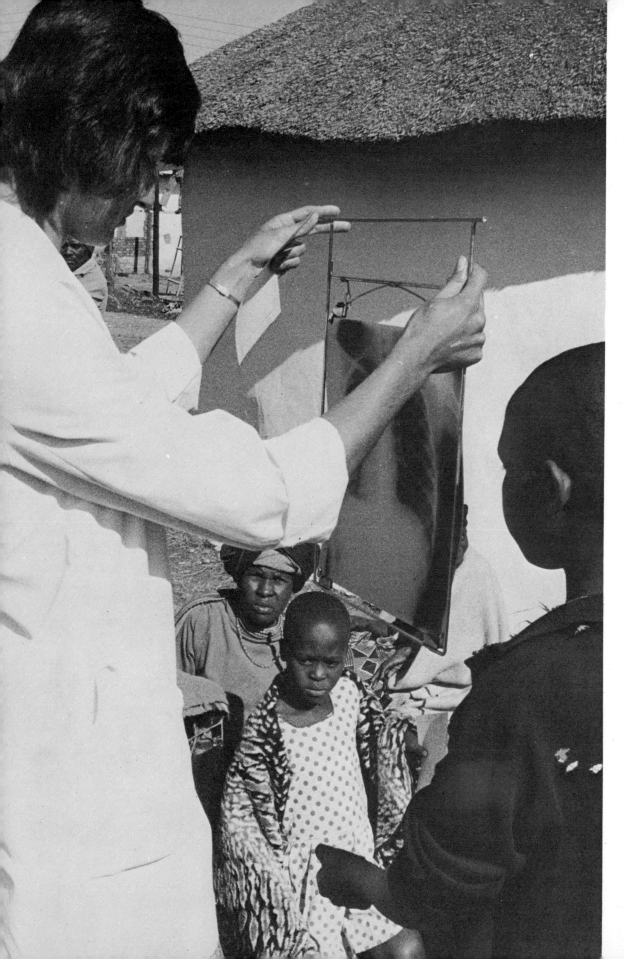

23, 24 + 25 At the outstations of the mission hospitals, as here at the Zithulele mission in the now independent Transkei, there is always much activity, especially when it comes to preventive treatment

26 + 27 X-ray is the first step in combating tuberculosis

26 **↓23**

25

technology

There have always been missionaries who have understood how to apply modern technical aids in the service of their work. Thus a number of institutions have been developed over the years which spread the Gospel using the most modern technical equipment. One of these establishments in the service of the mission of the Dutch Reformed Church is MEMA (Modern Evangelistic Methods in Africa).

MEMA has an annual budget of R120 000 and produces tapes with sermons in Afrikaans, English, the Indian language Tamil, Portuguese, Xhosa, Zulu and 12 other African languages. Slide shows with taped commentaries are also being produced, and films. In addition, MEMA also handles the religious broadcasts of the Churches in Botswana over the shortwave transmitter of Gaborone. The mission has also been running modern printing works and publishing houses to spread knowledge and the Word of God.

One of the latest aids is probably the MAF (*Missionary Aviation Fellowship*). This institution is, at least in Southern Africa, entirely new and still in its infancy. It originated through the initiative of a number of pilots who, during World War II, became convinced that one can also use the aeroplane in the service of peace and God. This gave rise to aviation services for missionaries in the US, Australia and New Zealand, and now also in South Africa.

The mission groups in a particular area must first decide if it is practical to employ an MAF pilot. Only then is a pilot with a suitable aircraft stationed in that area and is immediately at the disposal of all the mission societies involved. The running costs are shared by all the missions, while any flight for a particular mission is paid for at a specific rate per mile.

In many instances the MAF is, as always, dependent on voluntary contributions by devoted Christians. Although its operating costs are much higher than the money in hand, the unselfish pilots of the MAF are adding a new dimension to the work of the mission. The Dutch Reformed Church, too, is making full use of this modern means of transport, specially in the Republic of Transkei and in the Ciskei.

A pilot, Hennie Steyn, who has already flown for the mission in the Sudan, Tanzania and Kenya, saw to it that there are landing strips at the various mission stations. Doctors, nurses, medicines, patients, missionaries and specialists can be carried in the shortest possible time over the still largely undeveloped Transkei.

Hennie Steyn has this to say of his work: "When I draw the balance in the evening I am happy and frustrated at the same time. Happy over the many people whom I could help (the missionary, the patient, the teacher) and sad over the people who could not reach their destination because I was not available. I hope that my thoughts will manage to inspire some people to do more for this institution, more for the aviation service of the mission and more for the search of a growing number of pilots who are willing to become flying messengers for Christ."

1

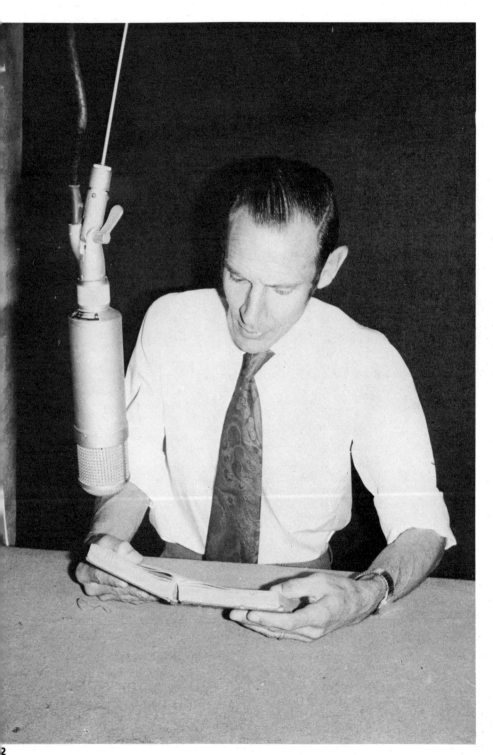

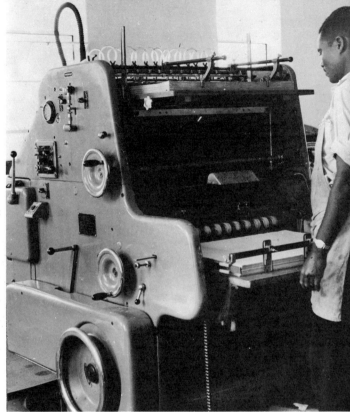

3

1 The mission realises albeit reluctantly that one can and must make use of modern technology to help spread the Bible message. Radio, film, television, modern printing presses and even the aeroplane are being mobilised in the service of the mission. Gersom Chipwaira of Malawi can still remember how it all began. On this old typewriter he typed the translated copy of the Bible in Chichewa from 1910 to 1918. The typewriter was a gift from a Cape farmer to the mission in 1903

2 Missionary A. T. Barry in Gaborone (Botswana) broadcasts weekly religious themes over Radio Botswana

3 Modern printing presses from Germany print mission literature and the Bible

4 In laboratories of mission hospitals gifted men and women are being trained

5 A linotyper at work

6 + **7** The D. R. Church's mission press in Bloemfontein, South Africa

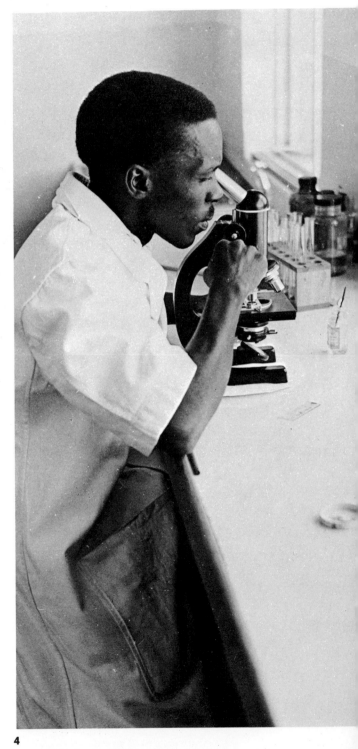

6

7

4

8 Women in the factory at Dimbaza

9 + 10 The most modern methods are also used to teach deaf-mute children

11, 12, 13, 14 + 15 The school for the deaf at Kutlwanong in Bophuthatswana, a homeland in South Africa, and its head, N. Nieder-Heitmann, have won worldwide recognition. World specialists come to South Africa to learn local methods. There are 10 institutions for deaf-mutes in South Africa today

10

13

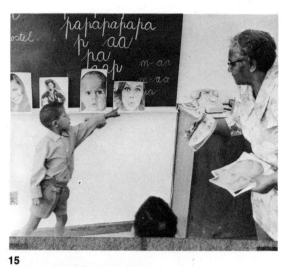

15

14

12
→

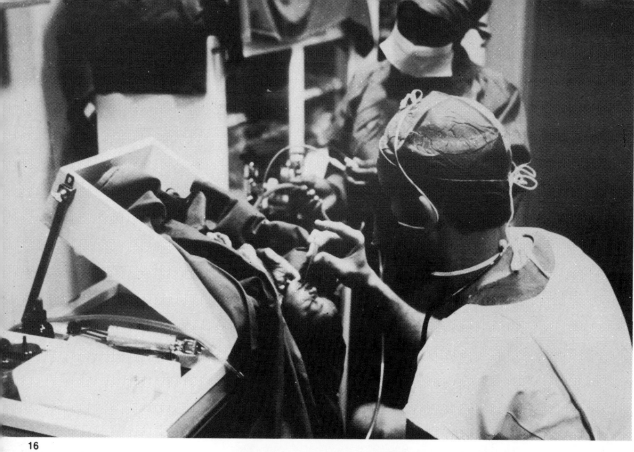

16

18
→

17

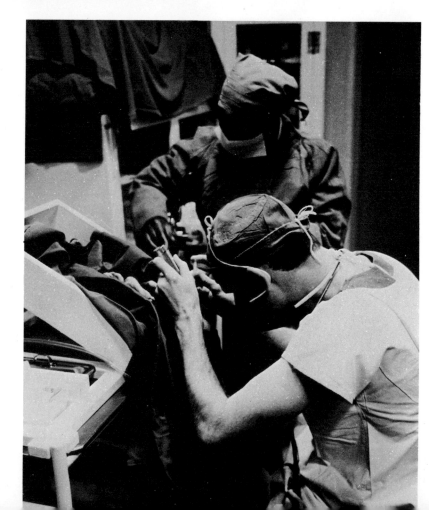

16, 17 + 18 The mission hospitals have
most modern equipment. In the hospital
Tshilidzini (Place of Mercy) in the Venda
of South Africa, White doctors take
care of a pregnant mother whose child w
delivered by Caesarian operation. Taking
care of the baby is the doctor's responsib

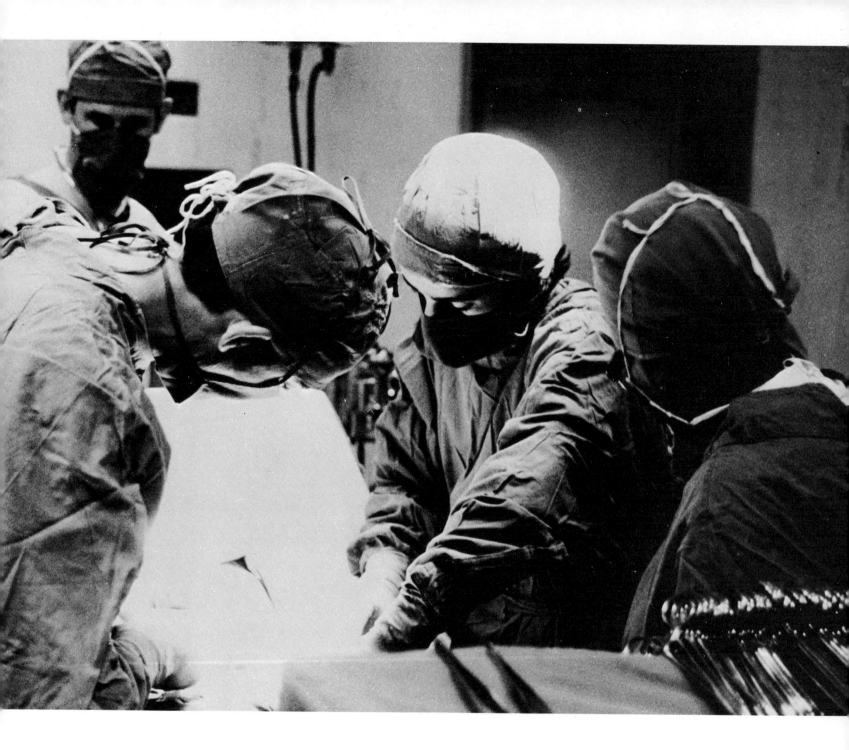

19 + 20 Windvane and -rose are the symbols of the mission pilots who now also do their fruitful work in Southern Africa

21 Symbol of modern technology and progress: The shadow of a mission plane over the huts of Transkeians

children

The mission of the Dutch Reformed Church has five children's homes with about 1 500 residents. Most of the children come from a-social circumstances (alcoholism among parents and divorce and child abuse are among the causes.) About five per cent of the children are orphans.

In these homes the children are cared for physically and spiritually. Schooling, recreation, sport and training in careers are included in the programme. Many girls are trained as shorthand typists and many boys as builders or farmers.

There are also six mission youth homes. There are about 1 000 pupils in these hostels.

There are, of course, a number of homes in South Africa in which sick or physically handicapped children are accommodated. One is Letaba, the showpiece of the mission. Letaba comprises seven boarding houses, eight school classes, a very fine dining hall, a modern kitchen, a handicraft hall and various workshops.

In Letaba there are on average 100 crippled Black children, who can be trained, 80 crippled children who cannot be trained and 60 seriously handicapped adults. The home is subsidised by the Ministry for Bantu Administration and Development while the Department of Bantu Education is responsible for the academic training of the 100 crippled children.

1, 2, 3 + 4 The mission pays special heed to the needs of children, particularly the handicapped. In Kwabadala, KwaZulu, children, caretakers and teachers enjoy a school outing with the blind and deaf-mute. Holding the hand of the White teacher they wade through a river for the first time

←
1

4

2

3

5

6

7

5, 6 + 7 The mission's nursery school in Botswana's capital, Gaborone, is the finest in the country where children find an opportunity for play, recreation and care. The children of many African diplomats are also gladly left in its care

8 Children, playing in the orphanage on the mission station Steinthal near Tulbagh in the Cape Province

9

10
→

9, 10, 11, 12, 13 + 14   The nursery school in Soweto near Johannesburg, South Africa, is, more than anywhere else, an important part of the mission work. After all, most of the parents work during the day and have no time to look after the children. That is why the children enjoy playing with paint and brush and regard a snack as a welcome break. The mission runs 17 nursing schools in the Transvaal

13

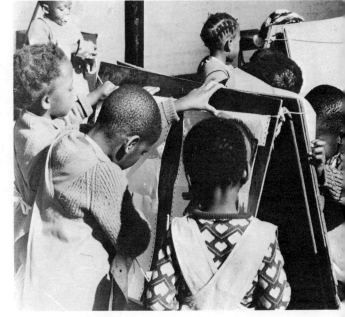

12

→
11

16

17

15 Children playing at the Witsieshoek Theological College

16 Deaf-mute children in KwaZulu

17 Children playing at Steinthal mission near Tulbagh

19

20

18

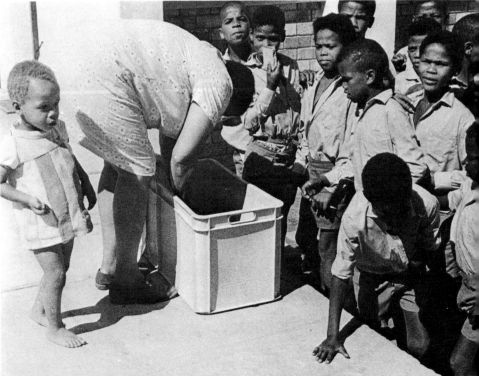

21
→

18, 19 + 20 In Efata, near Umtata, the capital of independent Transkei, blind children learn about the plants of their homeland. Education in the classroom is not neglected

21 The schoolbreak is welcomed and a small snack is handed out. At Steinthal near Tulbagh mainly neglected children and those coming from a-social environments are accommodated. They are mostly Coloureds from the Cape Province

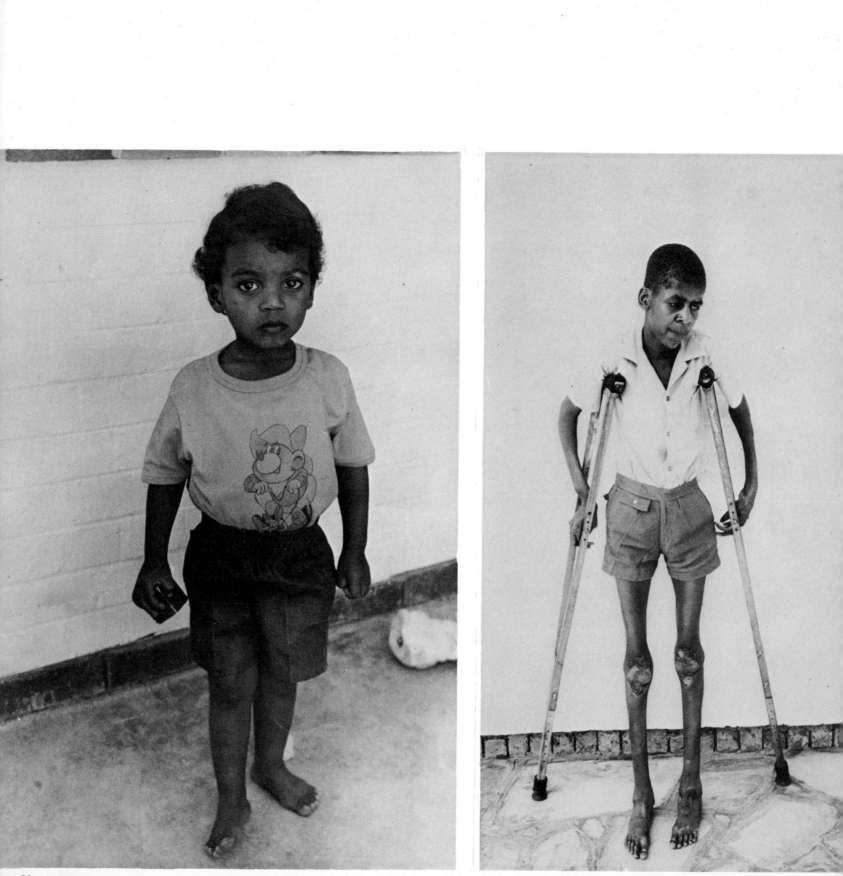

23   24

26

22
←

22 + **23** The *Nanniehuis* in Cape Town has become the home of unmarried mothers and their children. Over the past few years more than 500 mothers found sanctuary here and gave birth to their children

24 Also crippled children, like this Indian boy, find a friendly welcome and help in the mission homes

25 + **26** In the Cape, White girls of the Mission Workers' Organisation *(Sendingwerkersbond)* are intensely concerned with the education of Coloured children. Every weekend young people drive to the schools to busy themselves with the young ones

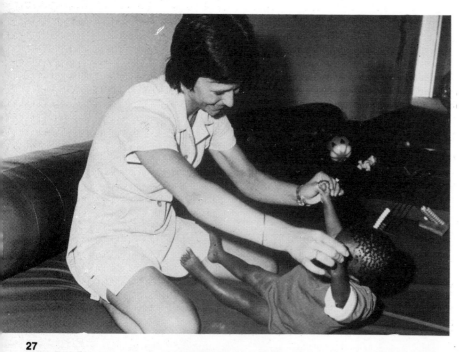

27

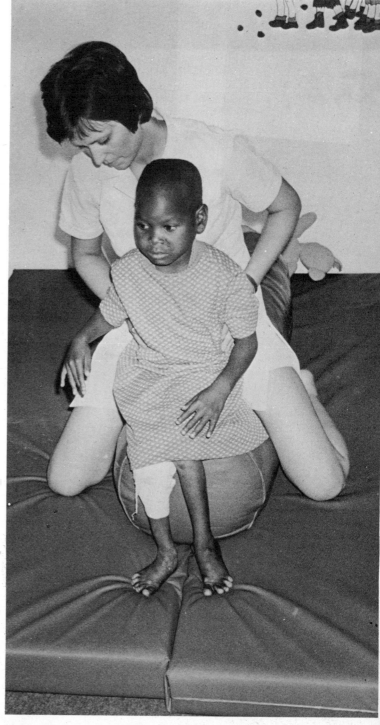

28

29

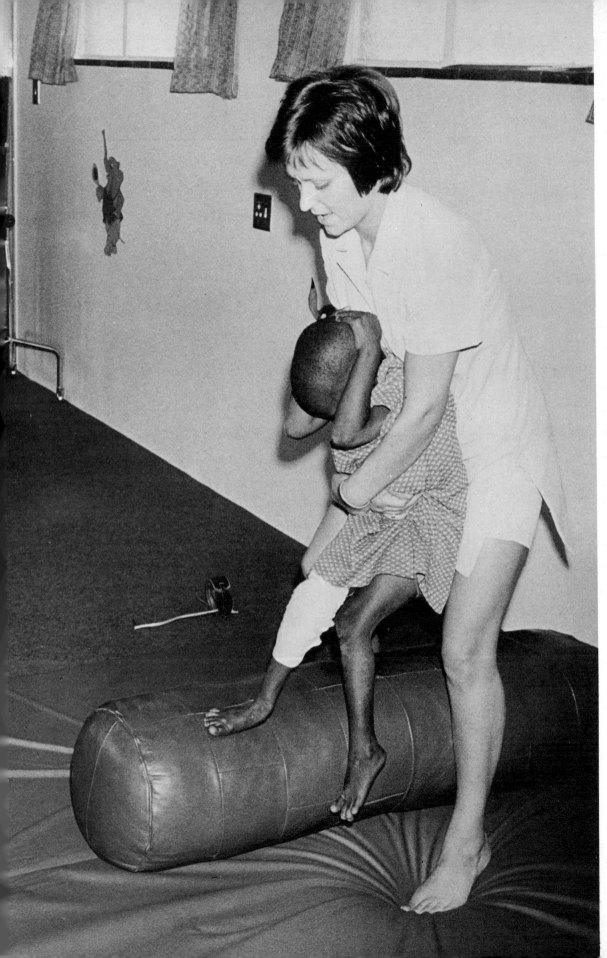

27, 28, 29, 30, 31 +32 In Letaba, Transvaal, a White nurse from Germany gives all her attention to spastic children. Tirelessly the various exercises are repeated. No child is neglected. The most modern equipment is available. And as thanks, a radiant and happy smile

←
30

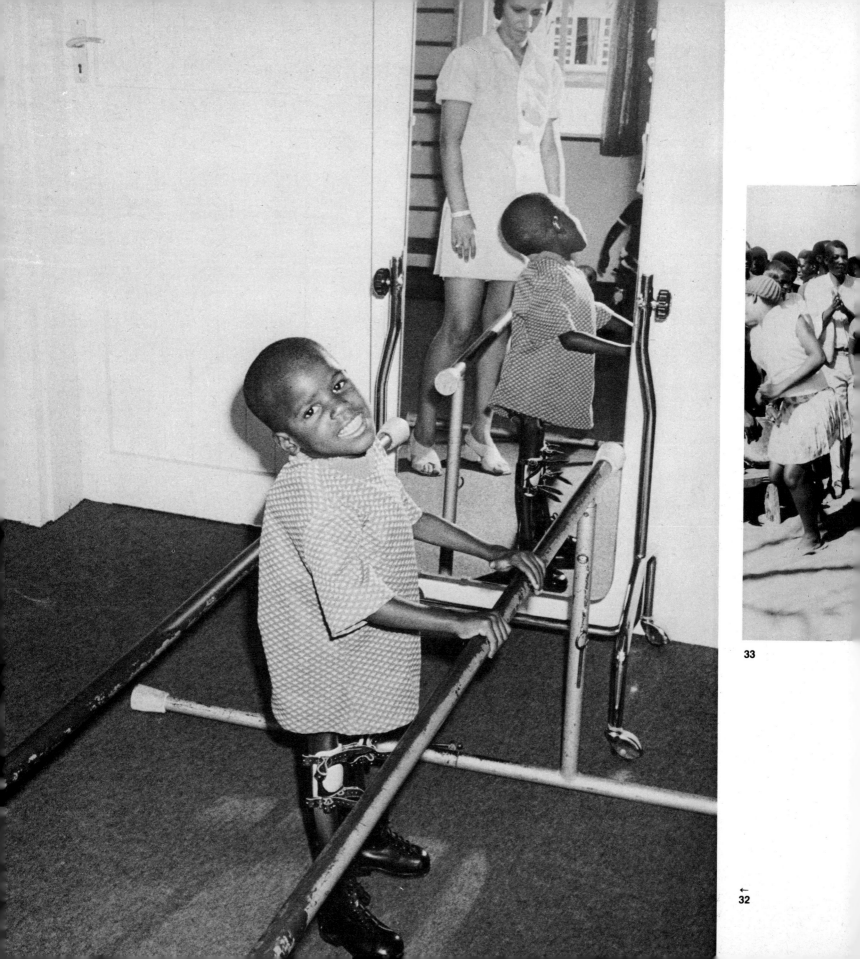

32

33

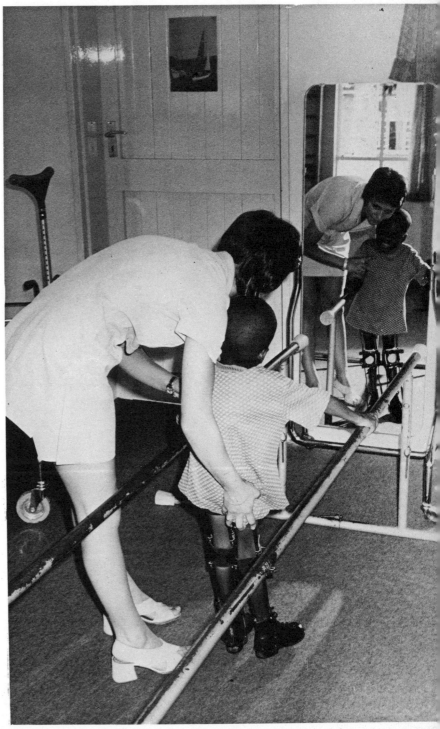

33 But gratitude, joy of living and happiness are not only expressed in smiles. Girls and boys of a mission station in Owambo (South West Africa) dance their native dances out of sheer joy

31

34

35

36
←

34, 35 + 36 The first school outing – a picnic in the open air with dance and play. For Whites this is nothing unusual, but in Africa it is an unknown and almost sensational occurrence

97

the blind and the mute

Once again figures next to the pictures will tell the story. In South Africa the Dutch Reformed Mission runs four schools for the blind with 383 Black pupils. Outside the Republic are two schools with 80 pupils. There is a total of eight institutions for the deaf with 718 pupils. One school cares for the blind who are also deaf and mute. There are 200 of these pupils.

There are five schools and institutions for 520 handicapped patients. A total of 625 old Black people are accommodated in five different old age homes. Chronically ill patients (505) are accommodated in six different homes. There is one home for people being treated for leprosy and discharged patients (216). Epileptics also have a home which is to be expanded to accommodate 750 patients.

The problem of unmarried mothers is well known among Blacks. Among Coloureds in the Cape it also plays a considerable role and a home for these girls has been built there. At present there is accommodation for 20 young mothers who, on leaving the home after the birth of their babies, may either take them or leave them behind at the home. Most of the babies are then adopted by married couples without children.

There are 17 créches for the children of working mothers which can accommodate 2 370 Black children. The Sunday Schools play an extremely important part in the work of the mission. In the young churches, 300 000 children — 50 000 more than in the white Dutch Reformed Church — are taught every Sunday. Between 1953 and 1962, 203 of the 213 new primary schools were built by the Dutch Reformed Mission Church (Church among the Coloureds). Up to 1962, the same Church administered 579 schools with about 70 000 pupils, i.e. 21 % of all pupils including those of the Government schools. According to the latest figures the Dutch Reformed Mission Church controls 633 mission schools with 75 000 children.

1 Special attention is lavished by the mission on the blind. This old man's greatest wish was a guitar

2 Deaf-mute children on a school outing in KwaZulu, homeland in South Africa

3, 4 + 5 Speaking exercises with a deaf-mute child, who feels the vibrations of a sound with its hands for the first time

2

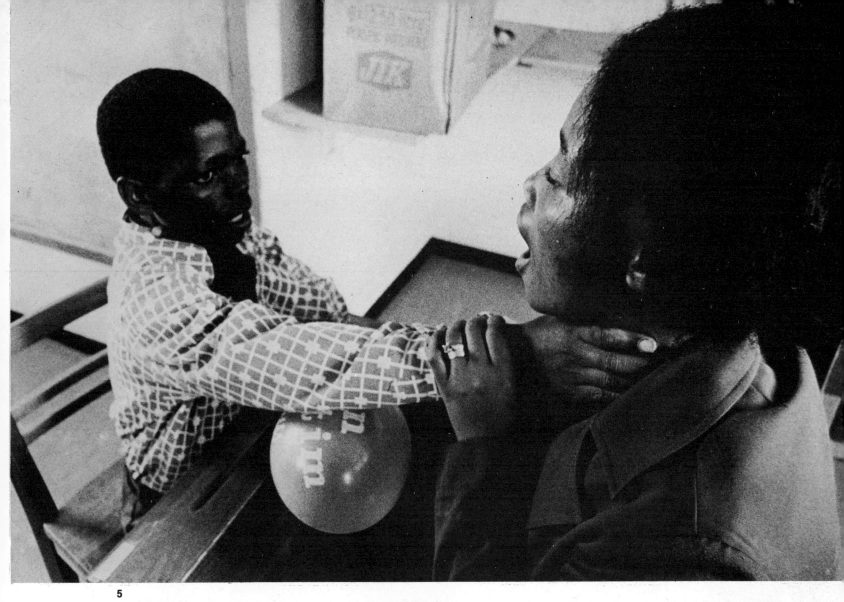

5

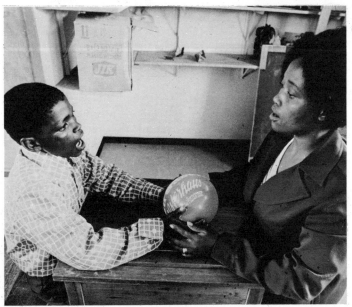

3

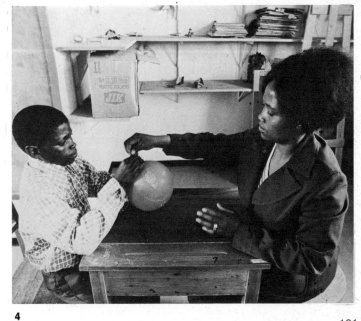

4

101

7

6 A deaf-mute child senses the vibrations of a musical note

7 Deaf-mute children show their drawings

←
6

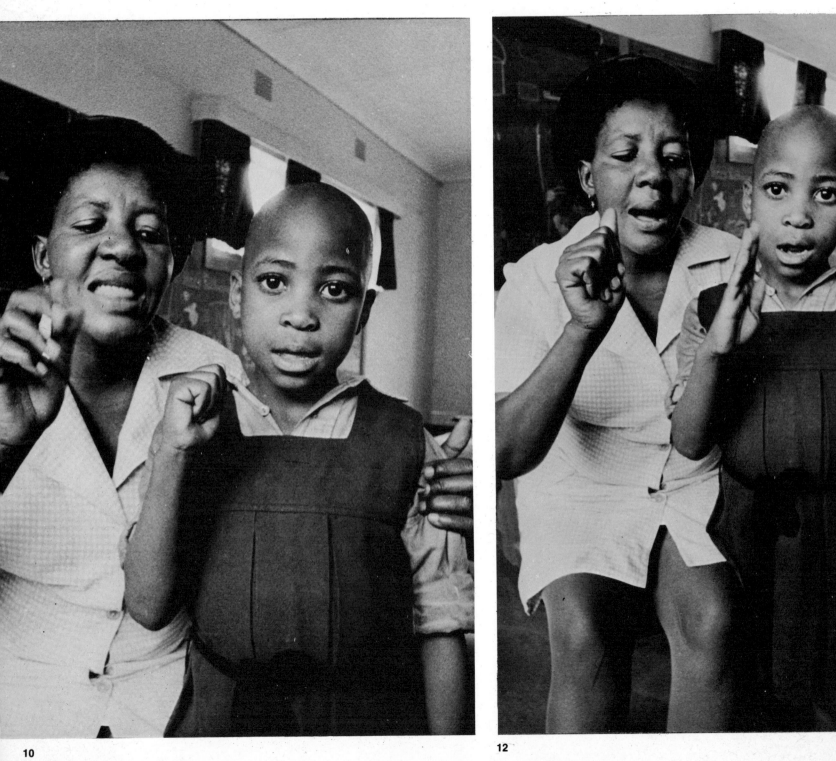

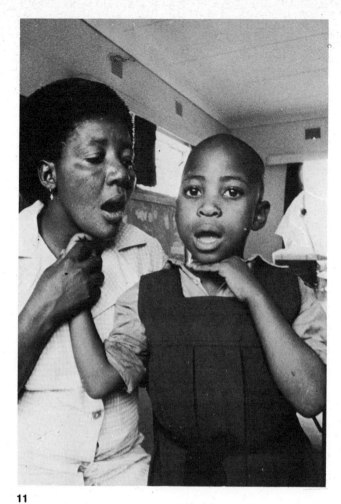

11

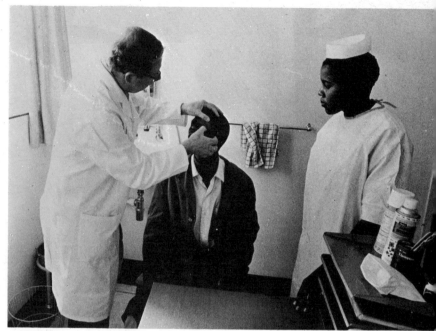

8

9
←

8 + 9 Eye diseases and blindness are among the greatest scourges of Africa. The mission doctors are particularly concerned with eye patients. Today, among South Africa's Blacks, there are 2 000 blind children who require special schools. By the end of the century the number of blind children may be about 5 000

10 The number of deaf-mutes and deaf-blind is also steadily increasing

11 + 12 In Kutlwanong, Bophuthatswana, education is particularly good. Last year more than 3 000 visitors, among them eight specialists from the USA, the Netherlands and Germany, came to study teaching methods here

14

education

The mission of the Dutch Reformed Church has always emphasised training. Sometimes the Church has led the Government in this field. There was, for instance, the situation in the Orange Free State when the Church was in charge of 40 % of Black schools. Later all the schools were taken over by the State.

The teaching curriculae were also started by the Churches and later taken over by the State. The technical training of semi-skilled labour was at first also done by the mission. At that time bricklayers, carpenters, furniture makers, gardeners, farmers and cattle breeders were taught at the mission. Women and children were trained in domestic science, childcare, weaving and rug making.

Everywhere in its missions the Dutch Reformed Church began with the building of hospitals, and the training of hospital and administrative staff (not doctors). In the Northern Transvaal the training of nurses in various hospitals is being done in conjunction with the Nursing College of Groothoek Hospital and at Rietvlei in Transkei.

A total of nine theological schools — five inside South Africa — takes care of the steady supply of ministers and evangelists.

1 + 2   The hunger for knowledge among the people of Africa is greater than ever. Here, too the mission of the D.R. Church is the bridge to modern civilisation. There is an enormous gap between the first reading efforts and the University of the North. The picture shows the university's library, which is in one of the most attractive landscapes in the Transvaal

3 Prof. P. G. J. Meiring during a lecture in Theology at the University of the North at Turfloop

4 Teaching deaf-mute children

5 Women in a factory at Dimbaza

4

3

5

6 + 7 Adults at a reading lesson in Malawi

8 Professor Elia Samuel Nchephe teaches at the Theological College at Witsieshoek in the homeland of Qwaqwa – one of the oldest mission stations in South Africa

9 + 10 Girl pupils in the Kaokoveld in South West Africa

6

8

7

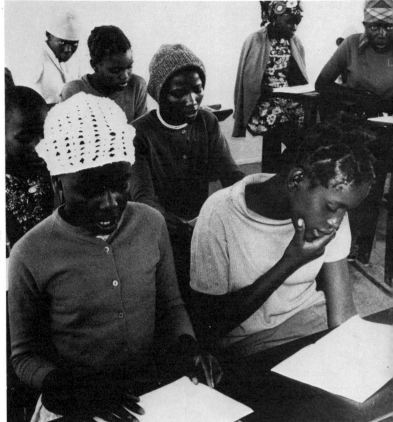

9

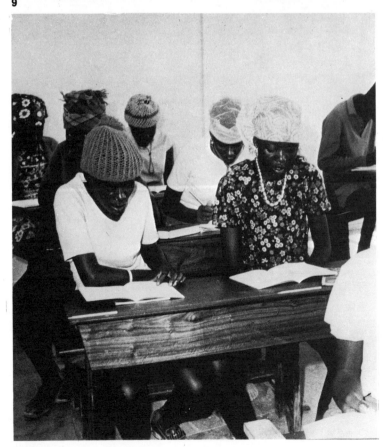

10

115

11 + 12 Training in basket making, a skill at which Black people are particularly adept

13, 14, 15, 16, 17 + 18 Great stress is laid on the training of hospital nurses. The willingness to learn is particularly great among the Black girls. All aspects of modern medicine are being taught. But the principles of modern office administration also have to be learned. The typewriter is part of that knowledge

11

12

↓14

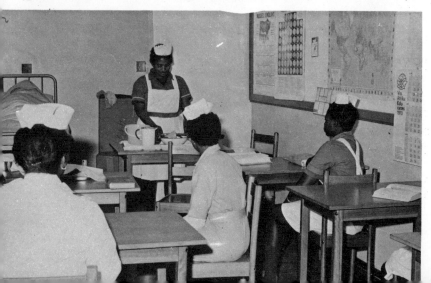

15

16

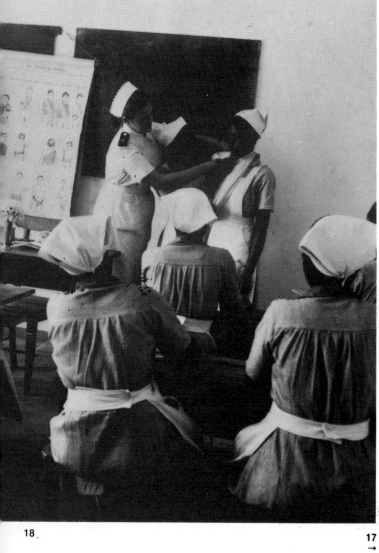

18

17
→

→
19

19 Hospital nurses welcome guests at the opening of the D. R. Church's Kgapane Mission Hospital with singing. The hospital is one of the most modern in the homeland of Lebowa. There are 257 beds, and 12 Whites and 142 Blacks take care of the patients

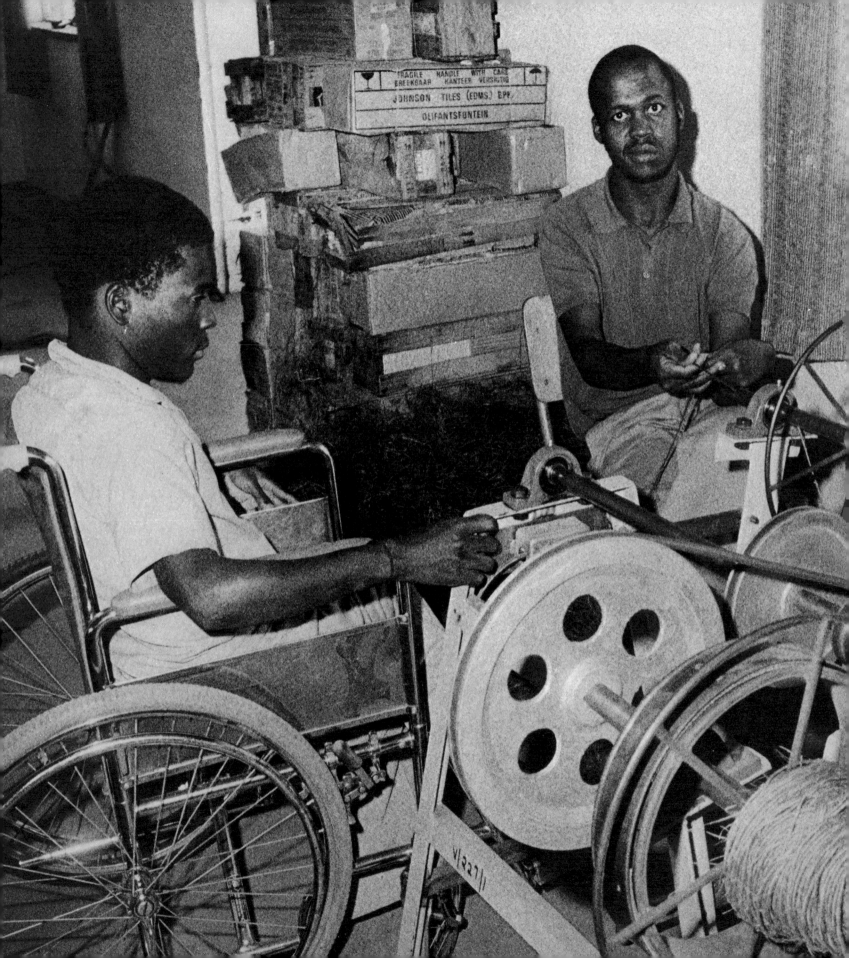

21

22 ←

20 →

20 In Mochudi (Botswana) young women are taught needlework

21 + 22 Letaba is exemplary in the training of sick patients. Under the guidance of the principal Mr. L. Booy, and his wife, they learn various handicrafts. What they make is later sold in aid of the home

121

23, 24, 25 + 26 A number of years ago Dimbaza received the attention of the world press. Seventy percent of the people had no work and were kept alive by donations. With the motto 'working hands are better than begging hands', the D.R. Church in Africa founded the Zipha Company, which today is concerned with the establishment of various factories. The first small factory in Dimbaza now manufactures spectacle cases and 40 women are employed. The aim of Zipha is 600 new jobs in Dimbaza, and for that it needs 919 500 dollars

23

24

25

26

evangelisation

Next to the offical helpers — the women and men who are wholly committed to the service of the mission — there is in Southern Africa a whole army of volunteers who dedicate themselves to the spreading of the Gospel, not only by their prayers; but also by their unselfish efforts during their free time at weekends. In the Dutch Reformed Church it is repeatedly emphasized that every member of the Church is a witness for Christ. An old pamphlet says: "You already begin to help if you treat all people with respect. You help even more by positively witnessing for Christ."

One can witness by talking to other people about the Bible and about Christ the Redeemer, but also through actual deeds.

Here the Church emphasizes in the first instance the attitude of the Christian, his behaviour towards the Black man, his manner of talking to him, the obligation to pay him adequately and to put a reasonable home at his disposal. Wrong actions and an unchristian attitude can have very negative results and can nullify the spreading of the Gospel. That is one of the principles of the Church.

With the aid of technology, especially audio-visual means, countless people are trying to promote the spreading of the Gospel. There is growing interest in the mission among students and other young people. At the University of Stellenbosch up to 600 students assemble almost every Sunday and spread into the surrounding country by bus, bicycle and motor-cycle to do mission work. At most universities one also finds more voluntary mission helpers who travel to the missions during their holidays to help with building and other activities.

Women's organisations are also playing an important part in the work of the mission. The women organise courses and prayer meetings with Black women. In Pretoria the Women's Mission Union has organised a maternity clinic with 97 beds for black women. The women's organisations spend more than 2.3 million dollars on mission work every year.

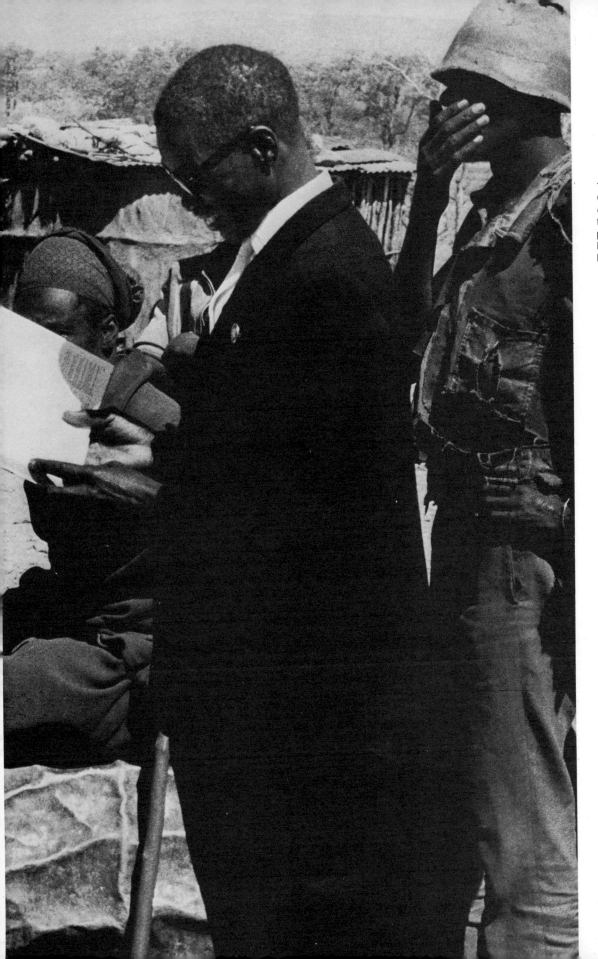

1, 2, 3, 4, 5 + 6 The spreading of the Gospel remains the goal of every missionary endeavour. The evangelists are tireless travellers. They bring the Word of God to people in the lowly huts of the Kaokoveld, in Kavango, in Botswana, in Rhodesia, and in the Republic of South Africa

←
2

4

6

3

7   Tree-church in South West Africa

8   Missionary Stander (Oom Flip) distributes Bibles

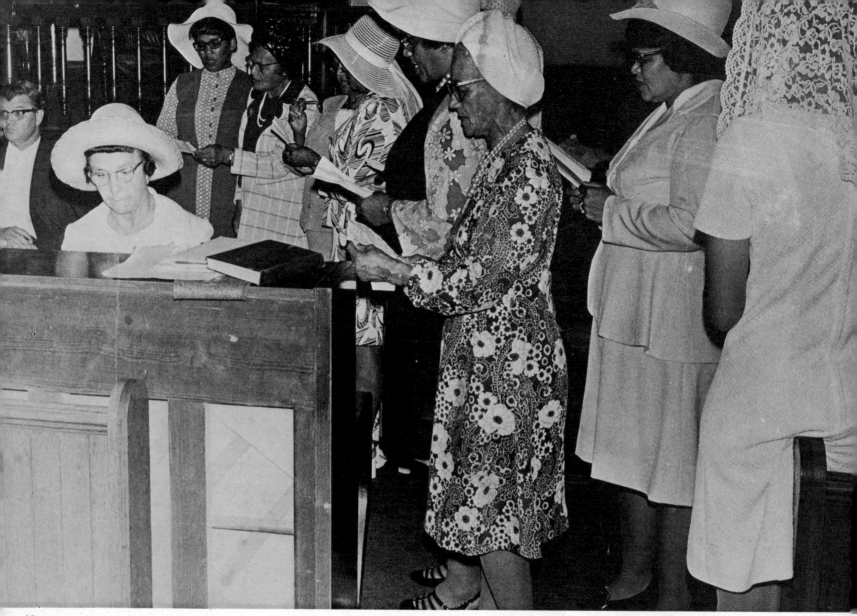

10

9↓

9, 10 + 11 In the country's oldest mission parish, the so-called *Suid-Afrikaanse Gestig, the Coloureds are still meeting, after nearly 200 years, for services and hearing the Gospel*

12 + 13 But also in the theological schools, like here in Turfloop or in Dingaanstat, the Word of God is taught and new ministers are ordained in the services of the Lord

11

12

13

15

17

14

16

14 The lepers near the Takuasa mission station also listen to the sermon

15, 16 + 17 Modern aids, such as simple record players and records with the Word of the Lord on them, the motorcycle and the world of the book, are used in the service of evangelisation

18

18, 19, 20, 21, 22, 23, 24, 25, 26 + 27 Students from the University of Stellenbosch and children from the humble quarters of Cape Town, travel to the mission areas, in buses, cars, on motorcycles and on foot. 'In the morning sow thy seed, and in the evening withhold not thine hand: for thou knowest not . . . ' (Ecclesiastes 11:6) is their motto. A total of 600 students travel by bus to the farms round Cape Town and 140 mission workers of the *N.G. Sendingwerkersbond* work every weekend in the Coloured townships. House visits, street work and Sunday schools are included in the programme. And for the children in the townships of Kasselsvlei, Uitsig, Elsiesrivier, Hanover Park, Kalksteenfontein and Guguletu, the arrival of the mission helpers is always a joyous day. The word of God is proclaimed. The Church is growing . . .

22

20

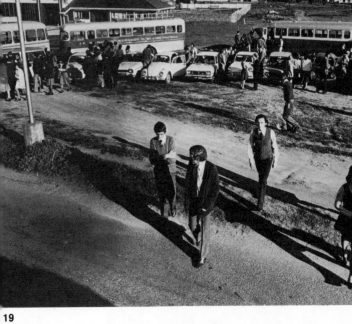

19

21

23

27

25

4

26
→

29

30

31

28, 29, 30 + 31 Praying children of the Tswana people near Saulspoort, The teaching professor in Witsieshoek (Prof. Elia Samuel Nchephe), and the man leading the prayer in the factory hall in Dimbaza are all engaged in the single, all-embracing task

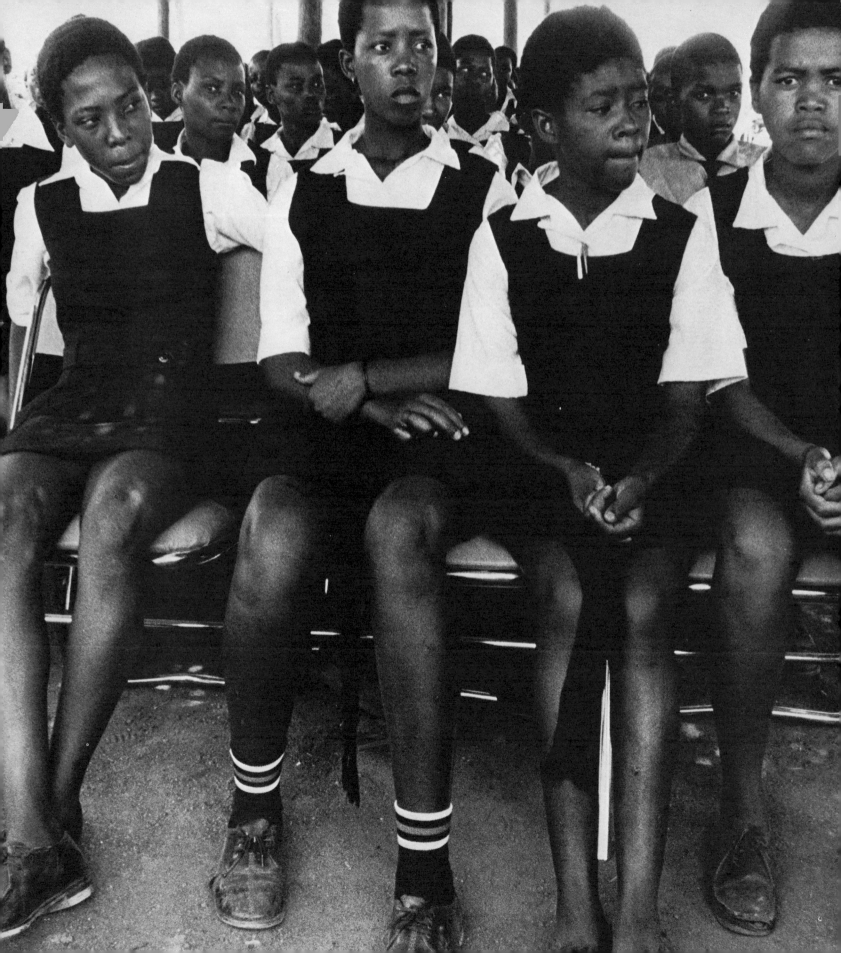

the church is growing

Enormous figures, inestimable sums. Almost every South African who is a member of the Dutch Reformed Church gives about R10 a year i.e. ($11,5), for the mission. But that is only one of his responsibilities. His own Church also requires certain offerings from him. Everywhere in the young churches new buildings are being erected which, as always, are largely financed by the D.R. Church. Only in rare instances, for example in the Coloured Townships of the Cape Province, do the faithful themselves finance the bulding of their churches.

In the young Churches today there are 844 parishes. Every parish has its central church building and often several smaller church buildings in the various outposts. At present there are no statistics available. The building of churches is proceeding at such a fast pace that one often does not have the time to register them centrally.

To spread the missionary idea and contribute to the growing church, a Christian Literature Fund has been established with a capital of 3.2 million dollars. The interest on this Fund is being used to promote the spreading of the missionary idea and Christian literature. It has a mission press and publishing house in Bloemfontein which prints and distributes Christian literature for the mission and young Churches. There are also mission presses at Morgenster in Rhodesia and Nkhoma in Malawi.

2

1
←

3

5

4

1, 2, 3, 4 + **5**   The Church is growing: Not only under the 'tree-church' in Kavango, where the Rev. W. A. Saayman is preaching the Word, but also in Malawi; not only symbolically and in the number of her members, but also materially in the number of churchbuildings

6 + 7 Almost everywhere congregation members lend a hand, give up their free weekends and sometimes also a couple of saved cents

8 Church in Mochudi (Botswana)

7

6

8

→ 13

9

14

9, 10, 11, 12, 13 + 14 Sometimes the missionary has to lend a helping hand, such as the Rev. E. N. Casaleggio, who carts water over many kilometers, or Rev. A. J. Botha and the Rev. I. J. Mentor in Rondebosch, or Rev. Jan Mettler in Hanover Park who, during weekends, climbs on the scaffold to build a new church for his congregation

11

12↓

10

15 Consecration of the church at Dingaanstat

16 Dingaanstat from the air

17

19

18

21
←

17, 18 + 19 The churches of the D. R. Mission are spreading over the whole of Southern Africa, from Decoligny and Zithulele (aerial photograph) in Transkei, to Nkhoma in Malawi, the headquarters of the Church there, to which today belong 68 parishes with more than 130 000 members

20 The Word of God is being preached

21 Holy Communion celebrated

20
→

22

22, 23, 24 + 27 Religious events are taking place, at which the women play a active part, as here in Bulawayo (Rhodesia) or the girls, as here in Malawi

25 New buildings are erected and old ones repaired

26 Congresses are held (Saulspoort)

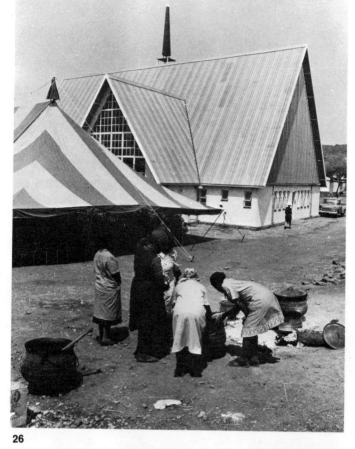

26

28 'I am a Sticker for Jesus'. Coloured choir in Cape Town

28

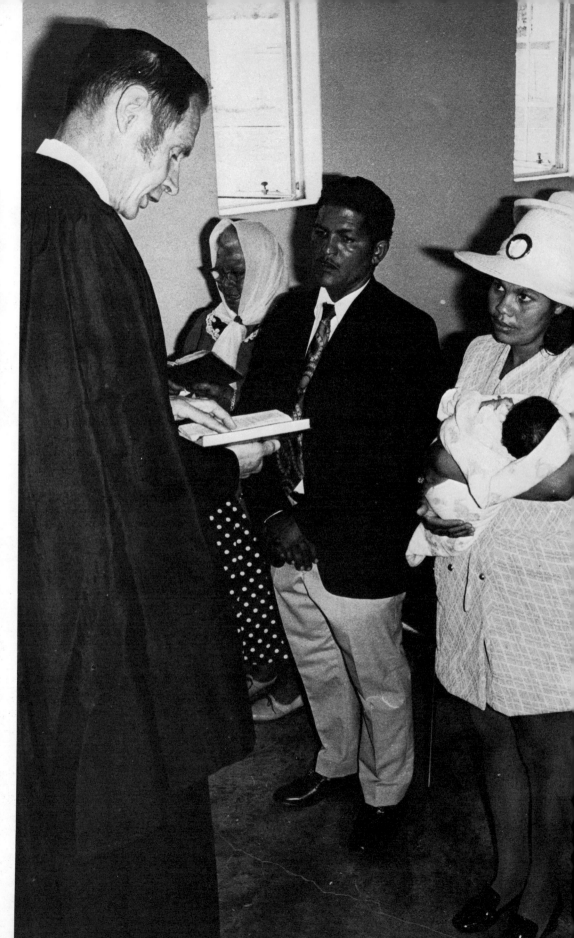

31

29   30
→

29, 30, 31, 32 + 33 New members are baptised . . . (Mochudi)

34 But above all stands the Word of the Lord: 'But go rather to the lost sheep of the house of Israel. And as ye go, preach, saying, the Kingdom of Heaven is at hand. Heal the sick, cleanse the lepers, raise the dead, cast out devils: freely ye have received, freely give' (St. Matthew 10: 6-8)

34